cook
without
a book
meatless meals

pam anderson

cook without a book
meatless meals

recipes and techniques
for part-time and
full-time vegetarians

photographs by quentin bacon

© 2011 by Pam Anderson
Photographs © 2011 by Quentin Bacon

Rodale books may be purchased for business or promotional use or for special sales. For information, please write to: Special Markets Department, Rodale, Inc., 733 Third Avenue, New York, NY 10017

Printed in the United States of America
Rodale Inc. makes every effort to use acid-free ♾, recycled paper ♻.

Book design by subtitle.it

Library of Congress Cataloging-in-Publication Data is on file with the publisher.

ISBN 978-1-60529-176-5

Distributed to the trade by Macmillan

2   4   6   8   10   9   7   5   3   hardcover

We inspire and enable people to improve their lives and the world around them.
www.rodalebooks.com

To Maggy and Sharon, my beautiful daughters
(and my fellow Three Many Cooks)

contents

introduction

The case against eating meat, poultry, and seafood has been building for a while. Many of us find it hard to stomach cheap, inhumanely produced factory farm animals and fish, yet wild resources are drying up, and local pasture-raised animals can be pricey and hard to come by outside of the farmers' market.

But go vegetarian? For years my standard response was: Not me. I love my food *my* way. Besides, I'm a food professional. I need to be able to eat what I want, when I want. Shouldn't I get a special pass?

That was my story, and I stuck to it for years. But eventually I started to feel like the smoker who continued the habit long after everyone else had quit. Finally, I couldn't ignore the issue anymore. It was time to stop *talking* like I cared about the treatment of animals on factory farms and all the ramifications of that system and start *eating* like it.

This internal debate came to a head one night while I was on vacation with my family. As the four of us sipped wine and picked at the remains of the paella we'd just enjoyed, the topic of factory farming came up. Everyone at the table acknowledged that it was an intolerable situation; the facts were unassailable. Like it or not, the way we eat—that is, the way our food is produced and transported in order to be sold to us at prices we'll tolerate—is not sustainable. Since no one was ready to go entirely vegetarian, we considered all the ways we could cut back on meat.

- **V(egan) B(efore) 6(pm)**
- **Vegan one day a week**
- **Vegetarian one or two days a week**
- **Daily reduction (but not elimination) of meat and fish consumption**

At first I argued for the drastic daily reduction of meat and fish consumption but quickly realized I'd forever be tempted to add a titch of prosciutto to the risotto, a bit of smoked salmon to the salad, or a little sausage to the sauce. I wasn't ready for a meatless life, much less one without cheese, butter, milk, cream, yogurt, eggs, and honey. Going full-time vegan or vegetarian felt premature—it was a way of life I didn't think I could sustain. I wanted to find something I really thought I could stick to.

But what about eating vegetarian two days a week? That I thought I could do. The quest for the best did not have to drive out the good. I could make a clear commitment to go meatless on Mondays and Wednesdays and buy only meat products that I felt good about—that were raised responsibly and sustainably—the rest of the time. Better for me, better for the earth.

Now two years later, what started off as a carefree conversation around a dinner table has actually turned into a way of life. It allows me to test recipes and eat as needed two days a week and gives me free rein to eat as I like on the weekend. The other two days of the week I can still fully partake of all the things I enjoy—

pizza, pasta, risotto, polenta, fruit, vegetables, nuts, cheese, olives, eggs, salads, stir-fries, pad Thai, and much more—just without meat.

And I'm not the only one who has made a permanent change to her meat consumption. My younger daughter and her fiancé have become committed locavores. They belong to a Community Supported Agriculture (CSA) group, shop weekly at farmers' markets, and get to know the men and women who raise the chickens, lamb, pork, goat, and beef they eat. All of their eggs and much of their cheese is local too. And because they pay dearly for it, they eat less of it.

My older daughter and her husband eat vegetarian—vegan much of the time—with serious regularity. And what started off as a two-day-a-week vegetarian way of life for my husband and me has spilled over into even more meals a week than the six we originally committed to.

But I've been at this long enough now to understand why so many people who attempt the vegetarian life can't sustain it. From fast food to fine dining, grocery stores to take-out and diet regimens, we're programmed to eat meat. If you want to eat less (or no) meat, you have to work at it.

For many, trying to go meatless cold turkey is akin to crash dieting. It's easy to envision eating vegetarian after you've just polished off a rich steak dinner, but after a few nights of cheese pizza, frozen veggie burgers, and

hummus, you'll quickly realize you're not equipped, nor do you know how to cook vegetarian. You may even think cooking vegetarian is just too hard. Who has time to spend all day chopping and prepping all those vegetables? It's so much easier just to throw a chicken breast on the grill, right?

To be a part- or full-time vegetarian for good, you've got to find a way to integrate the new way into your old life. Lots of people tell me they'd happily dial back their meat consumption; they just don't know how. Just as with weight maintenance, in order for your lower meat consumption to be real and forever, you have to make a lifestyle adjustment.

So what does an aspiring vegetarian need to stick to the commitment? First, you need a strong belief you're doing the right thing. Otherwise, you'll bail the moment you've got a "legit" excuse. Second, you need a decently stocked pantry, refrigerator, and freezer so you can live the life easily and spontaneously.

For part-timers, it's just a tweak. Start by buying less meat, poultry, and fish. As long as you keep adding it to your cart, you'll keep relying on it to get dinner on the table. You'll need very few meat replacements or special ingredients: just a few cartons of good-quality vegetable broth and miso, perhaps, or some tofu, tempeh, and seitan if you like.

It's more a matter of making sure you don't run out of common pantry ingredients like canned beans, tomatoes, quick-cooking grains, olive oil, vinegar, garlic, and onions—and most good cooking starts with these staples. It's also about keeping others, like fresh and frozen vegetables, eggs, and cheese, on hand in larger quantities.

Most of all, though, you need a set of quick, satisfying, easy-to-assimilate techniques and formulas that let you transform these simple ingredients into real meals. When it comes to dinner, most of us open the fridge and see a daunting mass of isolated ingredients. Take away meat—the easy anchor on most plates—and it's even more difficult to build an appealing meal. That's where *Cook without a Book: Meatless Meals* comes in. This book is set up to help you learn the skills and techniques you need to create fun, satisfying vegetarian dishes that feature the flavors and ingredients you like best.

With that knowledge and a decently stocked pantry, you can walk in the door and start cooking by heart rather than spend that time searching for a recipe full of ingredients you have yet to shop for. Without will, ingredients, and knowledge, it's very easy to revert to our carnivorous patterns.

I love recipes—I'm in the recipe business—but for everyday cooking, I believe recipes can often be a hindrance. Taking time to find a recipe, read it through, and check for ingredients are three hurdles you must clear before starting to cook. If you had a formula you just about knew from memory, you could start pulling ingredients and cooking almost immediately.

Most people I know love to browse at farmers' markets but often hesitate to buy because they simply don't know what to do with some of the ingredients. What if you could confidently pick up beautiful fresh produce because you knew several formulas you could slide those vegetables right into? Cooking this way allows you to create your own recipe based on the ingredients you've got—or want—rather than those you need to shop for.

Cook without a Book: Meatless Meals is divided into two sections, Not Strictly Breakfast and Fun Food the Rest of the Day. But one thing I've learned about the meatless life: There are fewer restrictions on what to serve when. Caesar salad with boiled eggs and hash brown croutons might be lunch, but it might also be dinner.

You'll find Cheesy Grits with Mushrooms and Smoked Gruyère in Not Strictly Breakfast, but pair it with an interesting salad and throw in a glass of wine, and you've got a very satisfying vegetarian dinner. And if you don't have time to enjoy a leisurely breakfast in the morning, make breakfast for dinner instead. Breakfast pizzas, Creamed "Chipped" Veggies on Toast, or Fancy Pancakes with an egg on top are all equally breakfast or dinner worthy.

And it's just as easy to turn dinner into breakfast. Frittata shows up in Fun Food the Rest of the Day, but it's very doable, even for a quick breakfast. Think strata is for brunch? In this book it's a quick, hearty dinner (though leftover strata is fair breakfast game in my meatless world). I can also vouch that

Weeknight Quiche (Pie for Dinner) and Six-at-a-Time Main Course Quesadillas (Fast-Food Favorites) recrisped in the toaster oven make very fun breakfasts too.

All these meatless formulas are simple, freeing, and work year-round. As long as you've got the base ingredients, you can make the dish with whatever ingredients you might have around. Love oatmeal? Turn the Master Formula into pumpkin oatmeal with warm spices and roasted pecans for the fall; prunes, vanilla, and walnuts in the winter; and blueberries, cinnamon, and roasted almonds come summer—or another combination that especially appeals to you. There's even a Black Forest version of this oatmeal whenever you've got a taste for a little chocolate and cherries.

Whether your tastes run sweet or savory, there's a formula for you—the Greek yogurt–based "imparfaits" can be made with either fruit or vegetables. The Wrap-and-Run breakfast sandwiches can be made savory with eggs, veggies, and cheese or sweet with cream cheese, fruit, and toasted nuts.

The breakfast pizzas swing both ways: vegetable-topped eggs and ricotta for savory tastes, honey-drizzled cream cheese and fresh fruit for those with a sweet tooth. There are savory and sweet pancakes too: Goat Cheese Pancakes with Peach Syrup or Savory Cheddar Pancakes with Chive Butter.

There are more fun formulas in Fun Food the Rest of the Day. How would you like to stir-fry without cracking a book? Or make pasta with any one of five different sauces and whatever vegetables you might have around? Or how about a galette or hearty quesadilla? It's all possible once you've taken a little time to internalize the technique or formula.

Of course there may still be times when you just want to follow a recipe, and there are certainly dishes that don't fit into a neat, tidy formula. For those occasions and dishes there are the Classics Made Meatless—all your favorite soups, salads, and sandwiches . . . without the meat. You won't miss meat in Black Bean Hominy Chili or the Meatless Cobb or even the Meatless Cubans and Potato Reubens. And you won't even miss the tuna with my Tuna-less Niçoise with Lemon-Feta-Dill Vinaigrette.

I don't see myself going full-time vegetarian anytime soon, but for now I'm willing to eat *less* meat so I can afford *better* meat. Along with millions of other cooks in this country, I want to see an end to the inhumane practices of factory farms. The only way to impact the supply is to reduce the demand.

I'm also willing to eat less meat as long as my meatless days are as satisfying and fun as the others. *Cook without a Book: Meatless Meals* finally means that's possible.

part 1
not strictly breakfast

I love breakfast. It's the first eating experience of the day, and it sets the tone for what's to come. If breakfast is fun, chances are lunch and dinner will be too. In fact, breakfast is about the first thing I think about when I wake up, and I love that I've got choices.

Because there are so many satisfying breakfast options, it's easy to forgo meat in the morning. I vacillate between sweet and savory; one week I'll crave eggs stirred into a mound of Cheesy Grits (page 10), then the next I'm on a smoothie kick (page 25). Just as quickly I'll switch to Greek yogurt Imparfaits (page 15), only to boomerang back to eggs, this time taking mine wrap-and-run style (page 31). Regardless of my whims, weekday breakfasts must be satisfying, varied, quick, and fun; and that's just the kinds of recipes you'll find in this chapter.

While there are ample options in the morning, the one thing no one has enough of is time, so I offer some shortcuts too. When there's a little more time, there are more options. By measuring the wet and dry ingredients the night before, Fancy Pancakes (page 57) become a delightfully feasible week morning meal. It's just like a mix—the batter's ready quicker than it takes to heat the griddle—except the pancakes are so much more appealing. How about Lemon Poppyseed Pancakes with Lemon Drizzle or Goat Cheese Pancakes with Peach Syrup (page 59)?

Think you have to visit a fine bakery for baked treats like chocolate and cinnamon scones (page 66) or bran muffins with cranberries and white chocolate (page 70)? Like Fancy Pancakes, pre-measured wet and dry ingredients means scones, and muffins, are ready for the oven before it's even had a chance to preheat.

Fruity or savory breakfast pizzas (page 39) fall into the category of special treat. For the weekend, make your own dough or stretch out store-bought. During the week, use the same quick, satisfying toppings on your favorite pizza crust, pita, or even naan. Want it sweet? Try a blueberry-almond pizza with honey–cream cheese. Need it savory? There's a cherry tomato and cheddar–topped ricotta version, just one of many delicious combos to try. And leftovers make a great on-the-go lunch.

So whether it's a grab-and-go morning or a lazy winter weekend, you've got a host of meatless breakfast options in this chapter, and there's nothing stopping you from heading over to Fun Food the Rest of the Day (page 72), where you'll find frittatas, quiches, stratas, and other satisfying breakfast and brunch possibilities.

oatmeal worth waking up for

A warm bowl of oatmeal with brown sugar, raisins, and a splash of milk feels dutifully virtuous. Oatmeal Worth Waking Up For is a whole new ball game. It starts with flavored soymilk, with dried or pureed fruit added to naturally sweeten the oatmeal as it cooks. (In fact, you shouldn't need additional sweetener unless, of course, you want it.)

The possible flavor combinations read more like a dessert menu than breakfast: imagine chocolate-cherry, pumpkin spice, figs and cloves (for Newton fans), or one of my favorites—oatmeal with prunes, vanilla, and walnuts. But do the math and you'll find that these naughty-sounding bowls of oatmeal are, in fact, very, very good for you.

master formula oatmeal worth waking up for

3 ½ cups chocolate or vanilla soymilk
2 cups old-fashioned rolled oats
Pinch of salt
Fruit (Pick 1)
Spices/Extracts/Zests (Pick 1)
¼ cup Nuts (Pick 1)

Combine the soymilk, oatmeal, salt, and **Fruit** in a large saucepan or 5- to 6-quart Dutch oven. Bring to boil over medium-high heat. (If using **Spices,** stir them in now.) Reduce the heat to medium-low and cook, stirring occasionally, to the desired thickness, about 5 minutes. If using **Extracts/Zests,** stir them in now; continue to cook for another minute or so to blend flavors. Serve sprinkled with **Nuts.**

Serves 4

oatmeal options

Fruit (Pick 1)

- 1 cup solid-pack unsweetened pumpkin puree
- 1 cup banana puree (about 2 ripe medium bananas)
- $\frac{2}{3}$ cup dried blueberries, cranberries, or raisins
- $\frac{2}{3}$ cup coarsely chopped dried cherries, peaches, apricots, dates, prunes, or figs

Spices/Extracts/Zests (Pick 1)

- Warm spice blend: 1 teaspoon ground cinnamon, $\frac{1}{2}$ teaspoon ground ginger, $\frac{1}{8}$ teaspoon ground cloves
- 1 to 2 teaspoons ground cinnamon
- 1 teaspoon ground ginger
- $\frac{1}{2}$ teaspoon ground cardamom
- $\frac{1}{4}$ teaspoon ground cloves
- $\frac{1}{2}$ teaspoon vanilla extract
- $\frac{1}{4}$ teaspoon almond extract
- 1 teaspoon finely grated orange zest

Nuts (Pick 1; buy roasted nuts, see notes and tips on page 6, or toast the nuts yourself, see page 270)

- Roasted pecans, coarsely chopped
- Roasted slivered or sliced almonds
- Roasted walnuts, coarsely chopped
- Roasted pistachios, coarsely chopped
- Honey-roasted peanuts, coarsely chopped
- Roasted and skinned hazelnuts, coarsely chopped
- Toasted coconut

pam's fave combos for oatmeal

Vanilla soymilk, pumpkin, warm spices, and pecans

Chocolate soymilk, banana, cinnamon, and peanuts

Vanilla soymilk, blueberries, cinnamon, and almonds

Chocolate soymilk, cherries, almond extract, and almonds

Vanilla soymilk, cranberries, orange zest, and pecans

Vanilla soymilk, golden raisins, cardamom, and pistachios

Vanilla soymilk, peaches, cloves, and pecans

Vanilla soymilk, prunes, vanilla extract, and walnuts

Vanilla soymilk, figs, cloves, and pecans

notes and tips

- If you have a container of premium roasted mixed nuts on hand, you can pick out ¼ cup of whichever nut you want when you need them (plus they're already roasted).

- Since banana and pumpkin puree are great in oatmeal, you might assume applesauce or apple butter would be too. Turns out they're not. Applesauce is not distinct enough, and the more concentrated apple butter is acidic enough to curdle even soymilk.

- You can use light soymilk, which has fewer calories, but I prefer the flavor and richness of oatmeal made with regular soymilk. I prefer soymilk to dairy milk because it's lower in calories, and of the nondairy milks, it's widely available and comes in chocolate.

- This recipe can easily be halved or quartered for 1 or 2 servings. If you like thinner oatmeal, stir in water at the end of cooking, or splash a little extra soymilk over the oatmeal once you've served it up.

- Spraying your knife with cooking spray makes it easier to cut dried fruit. ➤

great grits

When people say they don't like grits, I get it. At some point someone served them thin, watery, unseasoned corn gruel and called it grits.

The grits I grew up on were well-salted, peppered, and buttered and thick enough to sit on a plate with my bacon, eggs, and toast. I love 'em. So when people say they don't, I respond, "Try mine."

Over the years my grits have evolved. No longer are they a small side to a larger meal. They are, in fact, the main event. For this reason, I've exchanged nearly all the rich butter for bolder cheese. To add flavor and nutrition, I bulk them up with ingredients like tomatoes, peppers, mushrooms, or spinach—a delicious, early-morning way to sneak vegetables into your diet.

master formula cheesy grits

Scant 1 teaspoon salt
1 cup quick grits
Stir-Ins (Pick 1)
Cheese (Pick 1)

Combine 4 cups water and the salt in a large saucepan or 5- to 6-quart Dutch oven. Bring to a boil over medium-high heat. Whisk in the grits and **Stir-In** and cook, whisking, until the mixture comes to a boil. Reduce the heat to medium-low and simmer, partially covered and whisking frequently, until the grits are tender and thick, about 5 minutes. Stir in **Cheese**; cook until melted. Serve hot.

Serves 4

grits options

Stir-Ins (Pick 1)

- 4 cups (4 ounces) chopped spinach or arugula
- 1 box (10 ounces) frozen chopped spinach, thawed and squeezed dry
- 1 cup chopped tomatoes or quartered cherry or grape tomatoes
- 1 cup fresh or frozen corn kernels
- $\frac{1}{2}$ cup thinly sliced scallions
- $\frac{1}{4}$ cup finely diced roasted peppers
- $\frac{1}{4}$ cup finely diced sun-dried tomatoes
- $\frac{1}{4}$ cup (.25 ounce) finely diced dried mushrooms, your choice

Cheese (Pick 1)

- 4 ounces (1 cup) grated aged or extra-sharp Cheddar or pepper Jack
- 4 ounces (scant 1 cup) crumbled feta or goat cheese
- $\frac{3}{4}$ cup (about $1\frac{1}{2}$ ounces) grated Parmesan
- 4 ounces sliced or grated Gruyère, regular or smoked, aged Swiss, provolone or mozzarella, regular or smoked

variation: tomato grits with parmesan and basil

2 cups tomato juice
1 teaspoon dried basil
$\frac{1}{2}$ teaspoon salt
1 cup quick grits
$\frac{3}{4}$ cup grated Parmesan cheese
1 tablespoon butter

Combine the tomato juice, $2\frac{1}{2}$ cups water, the basil, and salt in a large saucepan or 5- to 6-quart Dutch oven. Bring to a boil, whisk in the grits, and cook until the liquid returns to a boil. Cover and continue to cook, whisking often, until the grits are tender and thick, about 5 minutes. Stir in the Parmesan and butter. Serve hot.

Serves 4

pam's fave combos for cheesy grits

Chopped spinach and feta (or goat cheese)

Provolone and roasted peppers

Pepper Jack and corn

Mushrooms and smoked Gruyère (or goat cheese)

Sharp Cheddar and scallions

Smoked mozzarella and sun-dried tomatoes

Fresh mozzarella and tomatoes (a couple of tablespoons of chopped fresh basil would make a nice addition)

Roasted pepper and pepper Jack (a couple of tablespoons of chopped cilantro would be delicious here)

notes and tips

- For more luxurious flavor stir in a small pat of butter along with the cheese.

- The recipe serves 4 but easily halves or quarters to serve 1 or 2.

- Dried and fresh herbs probably overcomplicate this hot breakfast cereal, but feel free to add a big pinch of dried herbs along with the Stir-Ins or a couple of tablespoons of chopped fresh parsley, basil, or cilantro along with the cheese.

- Grits aren't just for breakfast. Think polenta. Add a glass of wine and a salad and Cheesy Grits suddenly become dinner.

- Whisk the grits into boiling water gradually to prevent clumping and lumps. ➤

- Cheesy Grits and Eggs: follow the recipe for Cheesy Grits—any variation—stirring 4 large beaten eggs into the cooking grits after adding the cheese. ➤

imparfaits savory and sweet

With all the flavor and good looks of a classic parfait (but no tedious layering), these imparfaits, or relaxed parfaits, come in three varieties. For fruit fans, this breakfast-on-the-run can be made with nearly any fresh or dried fruit and your favorite nut or crunchy cereal.

For those with a taste for the savory, these same imparfaits can be made with cucumbers, tomatoes, or even grated carrots and topped with a little savory crunch: from crumbled bagel, pita chips, or seeded flatbreads to pine nuts or roasted pumpkin seeds.

Greek yogurt is the base for imparfaits. Not only does it boast 20 grams of protein per 8-ounce serving (compared with 13 grams in most standard yogurt), its stiffer consistency means these parfaits look smart on the plate. With all that protein, one of these paired with a piece of whole-grain toast will keep you satisfied until lunch.

master formula savory imparfaits

1 cup **Vegetables** (Pick 1 or more)
Salt and ground black pepper
$\frac{2}{3}$ cup plain Greek yogurt (0% or 2%, your choice)
Herbs/Spices (Pick 1)
1 teaspoon extra-virgin olive oil
Crunchy Topping (Pick 1)

Divide **Vegetable**(s) between 2 salad plates; season lightly with salt and pepper. Dollop each with a portion of yogurt; season lightly with salt and pepper. Sprinkle each with selected **Herb/Spice**, drizzle with olive oil, top with **Crunchy Topping**, and serve.

Serves 2

savory imparfait options

Vegetables (Pick 1 or more. Each of the quantities below yields 1 cup, so adjust quantities accordingly if using 2 or more, for 1 cup total)

- ½ large seedless cucumber, grated and squeezed dry
- 2 medium tomatoes, cut into small dice
- 1 cup grape or cherry tomatoes, halved—quartered, if large
- 2 medium carrots, peeled and grated

Herbs/Spices (Pick 1)

- 2 teaspoons minced fresh oregano or ½ teaspoon dried
- 2 teaspoons shredded basil leaves or ½ teaspoon dried
- 2 teaspoons chopped fresh mint leaves
- 2 teaspoons minced fresh dill
- 2 teaspoons chopped fresh parsley leaves
- 2 teaspoons minced fresh cilantro leaves

Crunchy Topping (Pick 1)

- ½ cup crumbled bagel chips
- ½ cup crumbled pita chips
- ½ cup oyster crackers
- ½ cup crumbled seeded flatbreads
- 2 tablespoons toasted pine nuts (toasted in a small skillet over medium-low heat, shaking occasionally, about 5 minutes)
- 2 tablespoons roasted hulled pumpkin or sunflower seeds

master formula fresh fruit imparfaits

1 cup **Fresh Fruit** (Pick 1 or more)
⅔ cup plain Greek yogurt (0% or 2%, your choice)
1 tablespoon **Sweetener** (Pick 1)
Crunchy Topping (Pick 1)

Divide **Fresh Fruit** between 2 bowls; top each with a portion of yogurt, drizzle with **Sweetener,** and sprinkle with **Crunchy Topping.**

Serves 2

fresh fruit imparfait options

Fresh Fruit (Pick 1 or more. Each of the quantities below yields 1 cup, so adjust quantities accordingly if using 2 or more, for 1 cup total)

- 3 kiwis—peeled and cut into small dice
- 1 large banana—thinly sliced
- ½ medium mango—peeled and cut into small dice
- Blackberries, blueberries, or raspberries
- Strawberries—thinly sliced
- 1 medium apple—cut into small dice
- 1 pear—cut into small dice
- Pineapple—peeled, cored, and cut into small dice
- 1 large peach (peeled) or nectarine—cut into small dice
- 2 large plums—cut into small dice
- Red or green grapes
- Figs, quartered

Sweetener (Pick 1)

- Honey
- Maple syrup
- Agave nectar
- Golden syrup
- Molasses (use only with apples and bananas or raisins and prunes)

Crunchy Topping (Pick 1)

- ½ cup homemade or store-bought granola
- ½ cup crumbled sweet bagel chips (such as cinnamon-raisin)
- ½ cup crumbled graham crackers
- 2 tablespoons coarsely chopped honey-roasted peanuts or almonds
- 2 tablespoons coarsely chopped candied pecans or other candied nut
- 2 tablespoons coarsely chopped roasted* nuts: hazelnuts, walnuts, pecans, pistachios, almonds (slivered and sliced work too), pine nuts
- 2 tablespoons toasted coconut*
- 2 tablespoons Grape-Nuts cereal

See page 270 for tips on toasting nuts and coconut.

master formula dried fruit imparfaits

1 cup Greek yogurt (0% or 2%)
3 teaspoons Sweetener (Pick 1)
½ cup Dried Fruit (Pick 1 or more)
Crunchy Topping (Pick 1)

Divide yogurt between 2 bowls; drizzle each with 1 teaspoon Sweetener. Sprinkle with Dried Fruit and Crunchy Topping. Drizzle each with another ½ teaspoon Sweetener and serve.

Serves 2

dried fruit imparfait options

Dried Fruit (Pick 1 or more; you'll need $\frac{1}{2}$ cup total)

- Blueberries
- Cherries
- Prunes, chopped
- Apricots or peaches, chopped
- Figs, chopped
- Dates, chopped
- Raisins, golden or dark
- Cranberries

Sweetener (Pick 1)

- Honey
- Maple syrup
- Agave nectar
- Golden syrup
- Molasses (use only with apples and bananas or raisins and prunes)

Crunchy Topping (Pick 1)

- $\frac{1}{2}$ cup homemade or store-bought granola
- $\frac{1}{2}$ cup crumbled sweet bagel chips (such as cinnamon-raisin)
- $\frac{1}{2}$ cup crumbled graham crackers
- 2 tablespoons coarsely chopped honey-roasted peanuts or almonds
- 2 tablespoons coarsely chopped candied pecans or other candied nut
- 2 tablespoons coarsely chopped roasted* nuts: hazelnuts, walnuts, pecans, pistachios, almonds (slivered and sliced work too), pine nuts
- 2 tablespoons toasted coconut*
- 2 tablespoons or more Grape-Nuts cereal

See page 270 for tips on toasting nuts and coconut.

pam's fave combos for savory imparfaits

Tomatoes, oregano, and seeded flatbreads

Grape tomatoes, basil, and toasted pine nuts

Carrots, cilantro, and roasted pumpkin seeds

Tomatoes, cilantro, and bagel chips

Cucumber, mint, and pita chips

Carrot, dill, and seeded flatbreads

Grape tomatoes, parsley, and oyster crackers

fresh fruit imparfaits

Pineapple and coconut

Mango and honey-roasted peanuts

Apple and hazelnuts

Banana and Grape-Nuts

Grapes and walnuts

Apricots and pistachios

Peaches and candied pecans

Strawberries and granola

Figs and pine nuts

dried fruit imparfaits

Dates and Grape-Nuts

Cherries and coconut

Raisins and graham crackers

Blueberries and toasted almonds

Prunes and walnuts with molasses or golden syrup

Apricots and pistachios

Cranberries and toasted pecans

notes and tips

- When using a moist vegetable like cucumber in a savory imparfait, press in a sieve to remove excess liquid. ➤

- Cut mango away from the pit for a fresh fruit imparfait, score the flesh, and invert to separate the cubes, then slice from the skin. ➤

anytime-good-for-you blizzards

Smoothies are good, but Anytime-Good-for-You Blizzards are even better—Strawberry Shortcake, Black Forest, Piña Colada, Chocolate-Banana–Peanut Butter Cup, S'more, Amaretti, Georgia Peach. All you need is soymilk, a frozen banana, frozen fruit, Greek yogurt, and a stir-in that provides fun crunch and flavor in an otherwise smooth drink.

Using frozen fruit—whether store-bought or seasonal fruit you prepped and froze yourself—not only instantly freezes the drink, but it's already prepared as well.

If you think breakfast is a bit early for one of the lean, low-sugar cookie options—graham crackers, vanilla wafers, gingersnaps—just substitute $\frac{1}{4}$ cup of your favorite granola or other sturdy cereal and enjoy the cookie-infused versions for a late-afternoon snack or even a healthy dessert.

master formula anytime-good-for-you blizzards

1 heaping cup **Frozen Fruit** (Pick 1)
1 banana, frozen, cut into chunks
1 cup vanilla or chocolate soymilk
¼ cup 0% or 2% plain Greek yogurt
2 teaspoons honey or agave nectar
Flavorings (Pick 1, optional)
Stir-Ins (Pick 1)

Place **Frozen Fruit**, banana, soymilk, yogurt, honey or agave, and **Flavoring** in a blender; process until creamy smooth. Divide between 2 glasses. Top each with a portion of the **Stir-In**, letting each person stir in his own.

Serves 2

blizzard options

Frozen Fruit (Pick 1)

- Strawberries
- Blueberries
- Banana (for a banana-flavored drink, use another banana in addition to the one called for in the recipe)
- Dark sweet cherries
- Pineapple chunks
- Peaches
- Mango

Flavorings (Pick 1, optional)

- 1 tablespoon unsweetened cocoa powder
- 1 teaspoon vanilla extract
- $\frac{1}{4}$ teaspoon almond extract
- $\frac{1}{4}$ teaspoon coconut extract

Stir-Ins (Pick 1)

- 4 vanilla wafers, crumbled
- 2 whole graham crackers, crumbled
- 4 gingersnaps, crumbled
- 4 Famous Chocolate Wafers, crumbled
- 8 amaretti cookies, crumbled
- $\frac{1}{2}$ cup granola
- $\frac{1}{4}$ cup honey-roasted peanuts
- $\frac{1}{4}$ cup candied pecans
- $\frac{1}{4}$ cup toasted coconut*
- $\frac{1}{4}$ cup miniature marshmallows

*See page 270 for tips on toasting coconut.

pam's fave combos for anytime-good-for-you blizzards

Strawberry Shortcake: strawberries, vanilla soymilk, vanilla extract, vanilla wafers

Raspberry Granola: raspberries, vanilla soymilk, granola

Black Forest: cherries, chocolate soymilk, almond extract, Famous Chocolate Wafers

Piña Colada: pineapple, vanilla soymilk, coconut extract, toasted coconut

Chocolate-Banana–Peanut Butter Cup: bananas (2 total), chocolate soymilk, cocoa powder, honey-roasted peanuts

S'more: bananas (2 total), chocolate soymilk, cocoa powder (for more intense chocolate flavor), a combination of graham crackers and miniature marshmallows

Amaretti: cherries, vanilla soymilk, almond extract, amaretti cookies

Blueberry Crumble: blueberries, vanilla soymilk, granola

Georgia Peach: peaches, vanilla soymilk, almond extract, candied pecans

notes and tips

- Since it's naturally sweeter and lower in calories than dairy milk, and widely available in both vanilla and chocolate flavors, soymilk is my beverage of choice for this drink. If you prefer one of the other milks, feel free to experiment, knowing that you may need to add a little extra sweetener to compensate.

- As fruit comes into season, why not freeze your own? Place the prepared fruit (leave berries whole) on a baking sheet until frozen and then transfer to a quart- or gallon-size freezer bag, making sure to get as much air out of the bag as possible.

- Greek yogurt adds body (and a little extra protein) to this on-the-go shake. ➤

- Just a few lean cookies, crumbled, give a lot of textural interest without a lot of additional calories. ➤

wrap-and-runs

Whether you're on the go or just need a quick breakfast, these sweet or savory flour tortilla wraps for 4 can be made in about the time you'd wait in the drive-through queue. Plus they're better for you and cheaper too.

Savory Egg Wrap-and-Runs (page 34) rely on naturally quick-cooking vegetables like spinach, roasted peppers, sliced mushrooms, and cherry tomatoes to keep morning prep to a minimum. If you've got leftover roasted or grilled vegetables, this opens up even more possibilities.

For a fruit-centric breakfast, try Sweet Fruit 'n' Nut Wrap-and-Runs (page 32). Simply spread light cream cheese on a microwave-warmed flour tortilla, then add your favorite seasonal fruit and a sprinkling of nuts or cereal for a little crunch. After that, it's just like it says—wrap and run.

master formula sweet fruit 'n' nut wrap-and-runs

8 tablespoons (4 ounces) reduced-fat
  cream cheese (Neufchâtel)
4 flour tortillas (8-inch)
2 cups Fruit (Pick 1 or more)
2 teaspoons honey or agave nectar
¼ cup Nuts (Pick 1)

Place 2 tablespoons cream cheese on each tortilla and, working 2 at a time, microwave until the tortillas are warm and the cream cheese softens slightly, about 15 seconds. Spread the cream cheese over the tortillas. Stir together the Fruit and honey and arrange one-quarter down the center of each tortilla. Sprinkle with Nuts. Fold in the sides of each tortilla and roll into a tight cylinder, burrito-style.

Serves 4

sweet wrap-and-runs options

Fruit (Pick 1 or more for 2 cups total)

- Strawberries—thinly sliced
- Blueberries, blackberries, raspberries
- Bananas—thinly sliced
- Peaches (peeled), nectarines, apricots, or plums—thinly sliced
- Apples—cut into medium dice

Nuts*: (Pick 1)

- Roasted (or candied) pecans or walnuts, chopped
- Roasted (or candied) whole (chopped), sliced, or slivered almonds
- Honey-roasted peanuts, chopped
- Roasted hazelnuts, chopped
- Roasted pistachios, chopped

*Buy roasted nuts or toast the nuts yourself; see page 270.

notes and tips

- Those with nut allergies can substitute an equal portion of granola or Grape-Nuts cereal.

- If you have a container of premium roasted mixed nuts on hand, you can pick out ¼ cup of whichever nut you want when you need them (plus they're already roasted).

master formula
savory egg wrap-and-runs

4 large eggs
$\frac{1}{4}$ teaspoon salt
Ground black pepper
1 tablespoon vegetable or olive oil
Vegetables (Pick 1)
1 scallion, thinly sliced (omit if using
scallions as your vegetable option)
3 ounces sliced Cheese (Pick 1)
4 flour tortillas (8-inch)

Adjust an oven rack to its highest position and preheat the broiler. In a medium bowl, beat the eggs with the salt and a few grinds of black pepper.

Heat the oil in a medium (10-inch) skillet over medium-high heat. When wisps of smoke start to rise from the pan, add the Vegetable and cook for the suggested time, stirring in the scallions for just the last few seconds.

Add the eggs; use a spatula to push back the eggs that have set and tilt the pan so the uncooked eggs run into the empty portion of the skillet. Continue pushing back the cooked eggs and tilting the pan until the omelet top is wet, but not runny. Remove from the heat; top the omelet with the Cheese slices and slide under the broiler. Broil until the cheese melts, 1 to 2 minutes. Slide the omelet onto a cutting board; cut into 4 wedges, halving each to create a strip and a smaller triangle.

Microwave the tortillas until warm, about 30 seconds. Place a portion of egg in the center of each tortilla. Fold in the sides of each tortilla and roll into a tight cylinder, burrito-style.

Serves 4

savory wrap-and-runs options

Vegetables (Pick 1)

- 4 cups washed baby spinach—cooked until wilted, about 1 minute
- 2 cups sliced mushrooms—cooked until golden brown, 3 to 4 minutes
- 1 cup halved grape or cherry tomatoes—cooked until softened, about 1 minute
- 1 cup drained and rinsed black beans—cooked until heated through, about 1 minute
- $\frac{1}{2}$ cup diced roasted red peppers—cooked until heated through, about 1 minute
- $\frac{1}{2}$ cup thinly sliced scallions—cooked until softened, about 1 minute

Cheese (Pick 1)

- Mozzarella
- Cheddar
- Swiss
- Provolone
- Monterey or pepper Jack

pam's fave combos for savory egg wrap-and-runs

Spinach and provolone

Mushroom and Swiss

Cherry tomato and mozzarella (sprinkle a little dried basil on the omelet, if you like)

Roasted pepper and Monterey Jack

Black beans and pepper Jack. Adding a couple of tablespoons of chopped fresh cilantro along with the scallions is nice, and wrapping up a bit of salsa in this one wouldn't hurt, either.

Scallion and Cheddar (omit scallion in recipe)

sweet fruit 'n' nut wrap-and-runs

Plums or strawberries and your choice of almonds

Apricots and pistachios

Bananas and honey-roasted peanuts

Peaches and candied pecans

Apples and candied or roasted walnuts

Mixed berries and candied sliced almonds

notes and tips

• Even if you're not cooking for 4, you may still want to make a full recipe of the eggs, which you can reheat in the microwave for a practically instant sandwich later in the week. But the recipe easily halves too—just make the eggs in an 8-inch nonstick skillet.

• Cook the vegetables until softened, then add the eggs to the pan. Use a spatula to push and lift the cooked eggs, allowing the uncooked eggs to run below. ➤

• Quarter the cooked omelet then cut each quarter into 2 pieces. Place on the tortilla and fold burrito-style. ➤

breakfast pizzas

When I think fun food, I naturally think pizza. And no, breakfast time is not too early to enjoy it—at least not these. Whether lovingly made from hand-stretched dough or banged out on a pita, these breakfast pizzas—both sweet and savory—are a beautiful way to start the day.

Need an eye-catching entrée at your next breakfast or brunch? Try Savory Breakfast Pizzas. Made from dough—store-bought or homemade, the choice is yours—they're rustic, beautiful, and classy. Just as important, they're quick and delicious too. The recipe makes 4, so it's easy to create different looks and tastes.

Fruit pizzas work year-round. When the weather's warm, make an array of summer fruit pizzas—plum, apricot, blackberry, and raspberry. For fall, bring on apple, pear, grape, and fig. For spring, showcase strawberries, mangoes, and pineapple.

Veggie breakfast pizzas offer variety as well. Make one of each—tomato, mushroom, spinach, and mixed bell pepper—and you'll never have to worry about who likes what. Plus it's a lot more fun and colorful to mix it up.

master formula savory breakfast pizzas

1 pound store-bought pizza dough (or ½ recipe Simple Pizza Dough, page 221)
Cornmeal, for baking sheet
1 cup part-skim ricotta cheese
4 large eggs
1 cup Vegetables (Pick 1 or more)
1 cup Cheese (Pick 1)
Herbs (Pick 1)
Salt and ground black pepper

Adjust an oven rack to the lowest position and preheat the oven to 500°F.

Cut the dough into 4 equal pieces and stretch each portion into rectangles about 12 by 4 inches, arranging all 4 crosswise on a large cornmeal-coated baking sheet. Spread ¼ cup ricotta over each portion of dough. Beat the eggs together with the Vegetables, Cheese, and Herbs, along with a generous sprinkling of salt and pepper. Pour the vegetable mixture over the ricotta.

Bake until crisp and golden brown, 10 to 15 minutes. Remove from the oven, cut into portions, and serve hot.

Serves 6 to 8

savory breakfast pizza options

Vegetables (Pick 1 or more)

- Mushrooms—cut into small dice
- Bell peppers—stemmed, cored, and cut into small dice
- Red onion—cut into small dice
- Frozen chopped spinach—thawed and squeezed almost dry
- Cherry or grape tomatoes—halved if small, quartered if large
- Scallions—thinly sliced

Cheese (Pick 1 or more)

- Goat cheese or feta, crumbled
- Mozzarella, Parmesan, extra-sharp Cheddar, Swiss, fontina, or provolone, coarsely grated

Herbs (Pick 1)

- 1 teaspoon dried basil (or 2 tablespoons chopped fresh)
- $\frac{1}{2}$ teaspoon dried oregano, Italian herbs, tarragon, dill, thyme, herbes de Provence, or red pepper flakes

pam's fave combos for savory breakfast pizzas

Mushroom, Swiss, and tarragon

Red onion, goat cheese, and thyme

Tomato, mozzarella, and basil

Red bell peppers (and/or scallions), extra-sharp Cheddar, and red pepper flakes

Spinach, feta, and dill (or oregano)

Mushrooms and spinach, goat cheese, and herbes de Provence

Peppers and red onion, Parmesan, and basil

Tomato and red onion, feta, and oregano

master formula fruity breakfast pizzas

½ cup (4 ounces) reduced-fat cream cheese (Neufchâtel)

2 tablespoons honey or agave nectar, plus extra for drizzling

Flavorings (Pick 1)

1 pound store-bought pizza dough (or ½ recipe Simple Pizza Dough, page 221)

Cornmeal, for baking sheet

2 to 3 cups Fruit (Pick 1 or more)

½ to ¾ cup Nuts (Pick 1)

Adjust an oven rack to the lowest position and preheat the oven to 500°F.

Microwave the cream cheese for 15 seconds to soften slightly. Mix the cream cheese with the 2 tablespoons honey or agave and the Flavoring.

Cut the dough into 4 equal pieces and stretch each portion into a rectangle about 12 by 4 inches, arranging all 4 crosswise on a large cornmeal-coated baking sheet. Spread the cream cheese mixture over each portion of dough. Top with Fruit and sprinkle with Nuts.

Bake until the crusts are crisp and golden brown and the fruit is bubbling, 10 to 15 minutes. Remove from the oven; drizzle with additional honey or agave, cut into portions, and serve hot or warm.

Serve 6 to 8

fruity breakfast pizza options

Flavorings (Pick 1)

- 1 teaspoon ground cinnamon
- ½ teaspoon vanilla extract
- ½ teaspoon ground ginger
- ¼ teaspoon finely grated lemon or orange zest
- ¼ teaspoon almond extract

Fruit (Pick 1 or more)

- Firm, crisp apple or pear—quartered, cored, each quarter halved crosswise, and sliced
- Fresh figs—quartered
- Apricots or plums—pitted and sliced
- Peaches (peeled) or nectarines—halved, pitted, each half halved crosswise, and sliced
- Strawberries—stemmed and sliced
- Blueberries, raspberries, blackberries (halved if large)
- Pineapple—peeled, cored, and cut into medium dice
- Seedless grapes—halved

Nuts (Pick 1; buy roasted nuts or toast the nuts yourself; see page 270)

- Toasted walnuts, pecans, hazelnuts, pistachios, chopped
- Toasted whole (chopped), slivered, or sliced almonds

pam's fave combos for fruity breakfast pizzas

Apples, hazelnuts, and cinnamon

Figs, pistachios, and vanilla

Apricots, slivered almonds, and orange zest

Strawberries, sliced almonds, and vanilla

Blueberries (or raspberries and/or blackberries), sliced almonds, and lemon zest

Pineapple (or peaches), pecans, and ginger

Grapes, walnuts, and cinnamon

variation: faster breakfast pizzas

By substituting 4 pita breads or 8-inch naan breads for the pizza dough you eliminate a big step and save even more time.

Adjust an oven rack to the lower-middle position and preheat the oven to 425°F.

Arrange the pitas or naan on a large rimless baking sheet (breads will overhang a little). Top as for savory or fruity breakfast pizza, and bake until the crusts are crisp and golden brown and the topping is bubbling, 10 to 12 minutes. Remove from the oven, drizzle fruity pizzas with additional honey, cut into portions, and serve.

notes and tips

• If you have a container of premium roasted mixed nuts on hand, you can pick out ¼ cup of whichever nut you want when you need them (plus they're already roasted).

• Use the back of your hand to stretch the dough into long, thin ovals. They fit better 4 to a pan, bake up crisper, and cook through more evenly. And they are easier to cut too. ➤

• An offset spatula makes it easier to spread the cream cheese topping. ➤

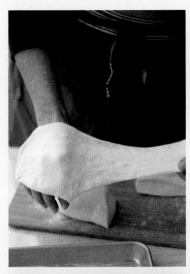

breakfast pizzas | 45

skillet potatoes and eggs

There's a breakfast spot my husband, David, and I hit now and again—Vera's Country Café—that combines my two breakfast favorites, potatoes and eggs, in one dish. Vera's Skillet Breakfast, a mound of tender-crisp potatoes with eggs scrambled right in, satisfies me every time.

Once I discovered you don't need to start with cooked potatoes to make the dish, it became a regular breakfast for me at home.

Serve it up and enjoy, knowing this dish will stay with you until you're actually supposed to be hungry again—lunchtime!

By the way, this dish is easy to double to serve 4 for brunch or a light dinner; just double the ingredients and use a medium (10-inch) skillet instead.

master formula skillet potatoes and eggs

6 ounces (4 small) red boiling potatoes, rinsed and cut into a smallish dice

2 teaspoons olive oil

1/4 teaspoon salt

Big pinch of **Dried Herbs/Spices** (Pick 1, optional)

3 large eggs, lightly beaten

1 scallion, thinly sliced

Cheese (Pick 1)

1 tablespoon chopped fresh herbs such as basil, parsley, cilantro, or dill (optional)

Combine the potatoes, 1/4 cup of water, the oil, and salt in a small (8-inch) nonstick skillet. Cover and bring to a boil over high heat. Cook the potatoes until the water has evaporated and the potatoes start to sauté, about 5 minutes. Uncover and cook the potatoes, using a wooden spatula to loosen them from the pan, until lightly browned, about 2 minutes longer. If using **Dried Herbs/Spices,** add them now.

Add the eggs and scallion and scramble until the eggs are just set. Sprinkle with the **Cheese** and optional herb. Turn off the heat and let stand until melted, a couple of minutes.

Serves 2

skillet potatoes and eggs options

Dried Herbs/Spices (Pick 1; optional)

- Oregano
- Basil
- Italian herbs
- Tarragon
- Thyme
- Herbes de Provence
- Paprika
- Ground cumin

Cheese (Pick 1)

- $\frac{1}{3}$ cup grated (or $1\frac{1}{2}$ to 2 slices) aged or extra-sharp Cheddar
- $\frac{1}{3}$ cup grated (or $1\frac{1}{2}$ to 2 slices) pepper Jack
- $\frac{1}{3}$ cup crumbled feta
- $\frac{1}{3}$ cup crumbled goat cheese
- $\frac{1}{3}$ cup grated Gruyère
- $\frac{1}{3}$ cup grated aged Swiss or $1\frac{1}{2}$ to 2 slices
- $\frac{1}{3}$ cup grated provolone or $1\frac{1}{2}$ to 2 slices
- $\frac{1}{3}$ cup grated mozzarella, regular or smoked or $1\frac{1}{2}$ to 2 slices

pam's fave combos for skillet potatoes and eggs

Pepper Jack and cilantro (serve with salsa if you'd like)

Feta and oregano

Goat cheese and thyme

Swiss and paprika

Extra-sharp Cheddar and fresh dill

Gruyère and tarragon

Provolone and Italian herbs

notes and tips

- Start with a few red boiling potatoes—just enough to more or less fit in a single layer in an 8-inch nonstick skillet. Dice the potatoes pretty small so they cook quickly, but they don't need to be diced super-tiny.

- Add the potatoes to the skillet along with a little oil, some salt, and just a bit of water and then cover. When the water starts to boil, set the timer for 5 minutes, and let them cook while you prep the rest of your ingredients. By the end of cooking time, the water should have evaporated and the potatoes should be tender and maybe even have started to brown.

- If you like, you can omit the scallions, but this perfect early-morning allium—no tears, no funky breath—provides great color and flavor.

- After the potatoes have steamed, give them a stir to loosen them from the pan, then sauté to brown. ➤

- Pour the eggs over the browned potatoes and cook briefly, then remove from the heat. Residual heat will melt the cheese and finish the eggs. ➤

creamed "chipped" veggies on toast

Chipped Beef on Toast, an often derided but secretly well-loved throwback to breakfasts of yore, is nothing more than thinly sliced salted dried beef rehydrated in a creamy sauce and ladled over warm, crisp toast. "Why not make a vegetable version?" I thought.

Broccoli, asparagus, and fresh mushrooms immediately came to mind—but this dish needed to be super-quick *and* feel like breakfast. Dried mushrooms were an obvious first choice—no sautéing—and they'd naturally rehydrate in the sauce. Frozen spinach was a natural as well, its liquid doubling as the vegetable broth in the recipe. Sun-dried tomatoes were a happy afterthought—a pinch of dried basil and this sauce tasted like Italy on toast.

You can top Creamed "Chipped" Veggies on Toast with a poached or fried egg—it's up to you. Either way, it's a great stick-with-you-till-lunch breakfast.

master formula creamed "chipped" veggies on toast

¾ cup vegetable broth (see Note)
¾ cup low-fat evaporated milk
Vegetable Toppings (Pick 1)
1½ tablespoons butter or olive oil
3 tablespoons all-purpose flour
¼ cup grated Parmesan cheese
3 or 4 thick slices whole-grain bread, toasted and halved

Microwave the broth, evaporated milk, and **Vegetable** in a 1-quart Pyrex measuring cup or bowl until steamy hot, 2 to 3 minutes.

Meanwhile, heat the butter in a large saucepan over medium heat. Whisk in the flour and cook until fragrant and golden, about 1 minute. Whisk in the warm broth mixture and bring to a boil. Reduce to a simmer and cook, partially covered, until the sauce is thick and the flavors are blended, 2 to 3 minutes longer. Stir in the Parmesan. If too thick, stir in 1 or 2 tablespoons of water to reach the desired consistency. Serve hot on the toast.

Note: If using frozen spinach, omit the vegetable broth; see Creamed "Chipped" Spinach, opposite.

Serves 3 to 4

vegetable toppings

Creamed "Chipped" Mushrooms

Use ½ ounce of your favorite dried mushrooms, chopped into small pieces if they aren't already in small pieces. (Like those magic animal capsules, they grow as they hydrate, and you don't want massive whole mushrooms floating in the sauce.) If you like, add a small pinch of dried thyme or tarragon to the heating milk mixture.

Creamed "Chipped" Spinach

Use 1 package (10 ounces) frozen chopped spinach. The liquid from the spinach will replace the vegetable broth called for in the recipe. Simply microwave the spinach on high until thawed, about 3 minutes, then add the spinach and its liquid to the evaporated milk. You should have a generous 2 cups. If not, add water to bring it to that 2-cup level. If you like, add a small pinch of grated or ground nutmeg to the heating milk mixture.

Creamed "Chipped" Sun-Dried Tomatoes

Simply add ¼ cup finely diced sun-dried tomatoes (if packed in oil, make sure to drain thoroughly) to the milk-broth mixture. Adding a big pinch of dried basil to the heating milk wouldn't hurt a bit, or try stirring a couple of tablespoons of chopped fresh basil into the finished sauce.

fancy pancakes

Pancakes are generally considered weekend fare, but they certainly don't have to be. Check out Fancy Pancakes. The ingredients list is short and the optional add-ins are intriguing. Just measure out the wet ingredients into one bowl and the dry ingredients into another the night before, and it's as simple as Aunt Jemima.

And while you're at it, perk palates with a little homemade fruit syrup. Sound time-consuming? It's not. Warm your favorite seasonal fruit in agave nectar or corn syrup and serve. Corn Pancakes with Blueberry Syrup (page 60) or Goat Cheese Pancakes with Peach Syrup (page 59) are two of my personal favorites. It really takes just minutes from prep to table, promise.

master formula fancy pancakes

1 cup bleached all-purpose flour
2 teaspoons sugar
½ teaspoon salt
½ teaspoon baking powder
¼ teaspoon baking soda
¾ cup buttermilk
1 large egg
2 tablespoons flavorless oil, such as canola or vegetable, plus extra for brushing pan

Combine the dry ingredients (flour, sugar, salt, baking powder, and baking soda) in a medium bowl. In a 2-cup liquid measuring cup, whisk together the buttermilk, egg, oil, and ¼ cup water.

Heat a griddle or large skillet over medium-high heat and brush generously with oil. Add the wet ingredients to the dry ingredients all at once; whisk until just mixed.

When water splashed on the surface of the griddle sizzles confidently, pour on the batter, about ¼ cup at a time, making sure not to overcrowd the griddle. When the pancake bottoms are brown and the top surface starts to bubble, 2 to 3 minutes, flip the cakes and cook until the second side is brown, 1 to 2 minutes longer. Serve hot.

Makes eight 3-inch pancakes

pancake options

Pumpkin Pie Pancakes with Toasted Pecans and Maple Syrup

Follow the recipe for Fancy Pancakes, omitting the ¼ cup water and adding ¾ cup canned pumpkin puree to the buttermilk mixture. Mix in ¾ teaspoon ground ginger, ½ teaspoon ground cinnamon, and a pinch of cloves to the dry ingredients. Sprinkle each portion of cooked pancakes with 2 tablespoons (½ cup total) coarsely chopped toasted pecans (see page 270 for toasting instructions) and serve with warm maple syrup.

Goat Cheese Pancakes with Peach Syrup

Follow the recipe for Fancy Pancakes, stirring in ⅔ cup crumbled goat cheese (about 3 ounces) into the finished batter. Serve the pancakes drizzled with Peach Syrup.

To make Peach Syrup: Bring ½ cup corn syrup and 1 cup sliced peeled peaches to a simmer over medium heat. Cook until the peaches release their juices and the mixture reduces to syrup consistency, 2 minutes.

Pineapple Pancakes with Warm Maple Syrup

Follow the recipe for Fancy Pancakes, omitting the water and adding ¾ cup crushed pineapple to the wet ingredients. If you like, drizzle these pancakes with warm maple syrup and sprinkle with toasted chopped pecans.

Brie Pancakes with Cranberry-Orange Syrup

Follow the recipe for Fancy Pancakes, stirring in a generous ½ cup (about 3 ounces) finely diced Brie into the finished batter. Serve the pancakes drizzled with Cranberry-Orange Syrup.

To make Cranberry-Orange Syrup: Bring 1 cup orange marmalade, ½ cup dried cranberries, and ½ cup water to a simmer over medium heat. Cook to a light syrup consistency, just a few minutes.

Granola Pancakes with Bananas and Maple Syrup

Follow the recipe for Fancy Pancakes, adding 1 teaspoon ground cinnamon to the dry ingredients. Sprinkle 2 tablespoons of granola (1 cup total) on each pancake as it cooks. Top each portion of cooked pancakes with ½ sliced banana (2 bananas total) and a sprinkling of extra granola. Serve immediately with warm maple syrup.

Lemon Poppyseed Pancakes with Lemon Drizzle

Follow the recipe for Fancy Pancakes, adding ½ teaspoon finely grated lemon zest and 1 teaspoon poppyseeds to the dry ingredients. For the lemon drizzle, mix ½ cup confectioners' sugar with ½ teaspoon grated lemon zest and 4 teaspoons milk and drizzle over the hot pancakes.

Corn Pancakes with Blueberry Syrup

Follow the recipe for Fancy Pancakes, stirring 1 cup fresh (or thawed frozen) corn kernels into the finished batter. Serve the pancakes drizzled with Blueberry Syrup. (For savory corn pancakes, serve with the Chive Butter, below.)

To make Blueberry Syrup: Bring $\frac{1}{2}$ cup corn syrup and 1 cup blueberries to a simmer over medium heat. Cook until the berries release their juices and the mixture reduces to a syrup consistency, a couple of minutes longer.

Savory Cheddar Pancakes with Chive Butter

Follow the recipe for Fancy Pancakes, stirring a scant cup (about 3 ounces) grated extra-sharp Cheddar cheese into the finished batter. Serve with a dollop of Chive Butter.

To make Chive Butter: Mix 4 tablespoons softened butter with $\frac{1}{4}$ cup snipped chives (or minced scallion greens) and a generous pinch of salt and ground black pepper.

notes and tips

- The batter should be thick but still fluid. ➤

- Flip the pancakes when the edges are set and bubbles form. ➤

savory corncakes

Serve these with a dollop of light sour cream (or even Greek yogurt) and drizzle with store-bought salsa verde (you'll need $\frac{1}{2}$ cup total) mixed with $1\frac{1}{2}$ teaspoons each: thin-sliced scallions, minced fresh cilantro, and fresh lime juice. To take the corncakes in a sweet direction, drizzle them with honey or your favorite syrup.

1 can (14.75 ounces) creamed corn
1 cup yellow cornmeal
2 tablespoons olive oil, plus extra for brushing griddle
1 large egg
$\frac{1}{2}$ cup bleached all-purpose flour
$1\frac{1}{2}$ teaspoons baking powder
$\frac{1}{2}$ teaspoon salt

Heat the creamed corn in a medium saucepan over medium heat. Stir in $\frac{1}{2}$ cup of the cornmeal to make a very thick pasty mush. Whisk in $\frac{1}{2}$ cup of water, then the oil, and finally the egg.

Mix the remaining $\frac{1}{2}$ cup cornmeal with the flour, baking powder, and salt in a medium bowl. Stir the creamed corn into the flour mixture until just combined.

Heat a griddle over medium heat; brush lightly with oil. Working in batches, drop the batter onto the hot griddle in $\frac{1}{4}$-cup portions. Cook, turning only once, until golden brown on both sides, about 5 minutes total. Serve hot.

Makes 12 corncakes

perfect scones, savory and sweet

Since meatless mornings should be celebratory, not austere, I offer the perfect scone formula, along with an array of fun, out-of-the-ordinary flavors, both savory and sweet. Ever come across a fig-and-goat-cheese scone? What about cherry-lime or cinnamon-chocolate? You'll wonder why you've settled for raisins all these years! Just follow the scone formula and pick your preferred variation, or use the variations as a guide to create your own special blend.

Scones may not be a regular on your weekday breakfast menu or a regular teatime treat, but they're simple enough that they could be. To make them quickly, do the prep work ahead. Mix the dry ingredients and grate the frozen butter, tossing it with a few tablespoons of the dry ingredients to keep the bits from sticking together before refreezing.

Thirty minutes before you want to sit down to warm scones, turn on the oven and work the frozen butter into the dry ingredients with your fingertips, adding the flavoring ingredients as instructed. Finally, mix in the wet ingredients, pat the dough into a round, and cut it into wedges. You should be finishing up just as the oven's preheated. While the scones bake, put on a pot of coffee or tea—scramble some eggs if it's breakfast—and then get ready to enjoy.

master formula perfect savory scones

2 cups bleached all-purpose flour
1 teaspoon baking powder
$\frac{1}{2}$ teaspoon salt
$\frac{1}{4}$ teaspoon baking soda
1 stick (8 tablespoons) unsalted butter, frozen solid
1 cup Cheese (Pick 1)
$\frac{1}{2}$ cup Flavorings (Pick 1)
$\frac{1}{2}$ cup sour cream (light if you like)
1 large egg

Adjust an oven rack to the lower-middle position and preheat the oven to 400°F. Line a baking sheet with parchment or nonstick liner.

Mix the flour, baking powder, salt, and baking soda in a medium bowl. Grate about one-third of the butter into the flour mixture on the large holes of a box grater; toss to coat with flour. Repeat the grating and tossing twice more. Using your fingertips, work the butter and flour together a bit more. Mix in the Cheese and Flavoring.

Mix the sour cream and egg with a fork until smooth. Add the sour cream mixture to the dry ingredients and stir with the fork until large dough clumps form. Use your hands to press the dough against the sides of the bowl to form a ball. (There may not seem to be enough liquid at first, but as you press, the dough will come together. If necessary, flick a little water into the bottom of the bowl to get the last bits to adhere.)

Turn the dough out onto a lightly floured work surface and pat into a $7\frac{1}{2}$-inch round about $\frac{3}{4}$ inch thick. Use a sharp knife to cut the dough into 8 wedges. Arrange the wedges about 1 inch apart on the baking sheet. Bake until golden, 15 to 17 minutes. Transfer to a rack to cool for 5 minutes. Serve hot, warm, or at room temperature.

Makes 8

savory scone options

Cheese (Pick 1)

- Grated extra-sharp Cheddar
- Crumbled feta, goat, or blue cheese
- Grated Parmesan
- Grated pepper Jack

Flavorings (Pick 1)

- Scallions—sliced
- Olives—green or black, chopped
- Sun-dried tomatoes
- Dried fruit: chopped figs, cherries, apricots, or peaches; or raisins or dried currants
- Scallion-herb mix: $\frac{1}{4}$ cup thinly sliced scallion greens plus $\frac{1}{4}$ cup chopped dill, parsley, basil, or cilantro
- Mixed fresh herbs: 6 tablespoons minced basil, parsley, and/or cilantro plus 2 tablespoons thyme, rosemary, dill, sage, and/or tarragon.

notes and tips

- Grating frozen butter creates uniform small bits that can be worked into the flour mixture without melting or becoming greasy. ➤

- Toss the butter bits to coat with flour then rub between your fingertips to combine, working quickly to prevent them from becoming too warm.

pam's fave combos for perfect savory scones

Cheddar and scallions

Feta and pimiento-stuffed olives

Goat cheese and fig (add 1 tablespoon minced fresh rosemary if you like)

Blue cheese and golden raisins

Parmesan and mixed fresh herbs

Fontina and scallion-dill mix

Pepper Jack and scallion-cilantro mix

master formula perfect sweet scones

2 cups bleached all-purpose flour
6 tablespoons sugar, plus 1 teaspoon for sprinkling (see Note)
1 teaspoon baking powder
½ teaspoon salt
¼ teaspoon baking soda
Zests/Spices/Herbs (Pick 1)
1 stick (8 tablespoons) unsalted butter, frozen solid
½ cup Flavorings (Pick 1)
½ cup sour cream (light if you like)
1 large egg

Adjust an oven rack to the lower-middle position and preheat the oven to 400°F. Line a baking sheet with parchment paper or nonstick liner.

Mix the flour, 6 tablespoons of the sugar, the baking powder, salt, baking soda, and Zests/Spices/Herbs in a medium bowl. Grate one-third of the butter into the flour mixture on the large holes of a box grater; toss to coat with the flour. Repeat grating and tossing twice more. Using your fingertips, work the butter and flour together a bit more. Mix in the Flavoring.

Mix the sour cream and egg with a fork until smooth. Stir the sour cream mixture into the dry ingredients with the fork until large dough clumps form. Use your hands to press the dough against the side of the bowl to form a ball. (There may not seem to be enough liquid at first, but as you press, the dough will come together. If necessary, flick a little water into the bottom of the bowl to get the last bits to adhere.) Turn out onto a lightly floured work surface and pat into a 7½-inch round about ¾ inch thick. Sprinkle with the remaining teaspoon of sugar. Use a sharp knife to cut into 8 wedges. Place the wedges about 1 inch apart on the baking sheet. Bake until golden, 15 to 17 minutes. Transfer to a rack to cool for 5 minutes. Serve hot, warm, or at room temperature.

Note: If you have some, coarse sugar is especially nice for sprinkling the scones before baking. If using coarse sugar, increase the amount to 2 teaspoons.

Makes 8

sweet scone options

Zests/Spices/Herbs (Pick 1 or 1 herb or spice plus a zest)

- 2 teaspoons minced fresh rosemary
- 2 teaspoons minced fresh thyme leaves
- 1½ teaspoons ground cinnamon
- 1 teaspoon grated citrus zest—lemon, orange, lime
- 1 teaspoon ground ginger

Flavorings (Pick 1)

- Semi- or bittersweet chocolate—chopped
- White chocolate—chopped
- Dried fruit: raisins (golden or dark), currants, blueberries, or cranberries; or coarsely chopped cherries, apricots, peaches, or strawberries
- Crystallized ginger—coarsely chopped

- Flick some water into the bottom of the bowl to collect the last bits as you gather the dough into a ball. ➤

pam's fave combos for perfect sweet scones

Chocolate and cinnamon

Orange zest and rosemary (omit the Flavoring)

Cherries and lime zest

Double ginger (both crystallized and ground ginger)

Strawberries and orange zest

Blueberries and thyme

big beautiful bran muffins

The name says it all. These muffins are indeed big and beautiful and mostly nice, with an option to make them a little naughty. They're substantial yet tender, sweet but not too much so. The ingredients list may look long, but the technique is standard quick bread—mix dry; mix wet; mix the two; bake and serve.

In addition to the bran, these muffins are chock-full of good-for-you dried fruit. You can stop there or add a handful of nuts. But I'm giving you permission to add a little chopped dark or white chocolate— just $1/2$ cup for the dozen—for something really special.

These muffins are likely to be weekend fare in your house, but like pancakes and scones, these can become easy weekday treats if you pre-measure the wet and dry ingredients the night before and do the final mix and bake the next morning. These muffins freeze well too, so bake a batch on the weekend, wrap the cooled muffins individually, and pull them from the freezer one at a time during the week. I know from experience they microwave to sheer perfection.

master formula big beautiful bran muffins

3 cups bleached all-purpose flour
1 tablespoon baking powder
½ teaspoon baking soda
½ teaspoon salt
Flavorings (Pick 1, optional)
2 cups low-fat plain (not Greek) yogurt
1½ cups unprocessed wheat bran
¾ cup packed dark brown sugar
½ cup plus 2 tablespoons vegetable oil
¼ cup unsulphured molasses
2 large eggs
1½ cups Dried Fruit (Pick 1 or more)
½ cup Extras (Pick 1, optional)

Adjust an oven rack to the lower-middle position and preheat the oven to 375°F. Coat 12 muffin cups (½-cup capacity) with nonstick spray.

Mix the flour, baking powder, baking soda, salt, and Flavoring (if using) in a large bowl. Mix the yogurt, bran, brown sugar, oil, molasses, and eggs in a medium bowl. Mix the wet ingredients into the dry ingredients to form a smooth batter. Fold in the Dried Fruit and Extra (if using). Fill the muffin cups with batter (a spring-action ice-cream scoop works well for this).

Bake until golden brown, 20 to 25 minutes. Let cool in the pan for a couple of minutes, then turn the muffins onto a rack to cool. Serve warm or at room temperature. (Muffins can be stored in a resealable plastic bag and frozen for up to 1 month.)

Makes 1 dozen

bran muffin options

Flavorings (Pick 1; optional, but good)
- 2 teaspoons finely grated orange zest
- 2 teaspoons ground cinnamon
- 1 teaspoon ground cardamom

Dried Fruit (Pick 1 or more for $1\frac{1}{2}$ cups in total)
- Cherries
- Blueberries
- Strawberries, chopped
- Cranberries
- Golden or dark raisins

Extras (Pick 1; optional, but good)
- Bittersweet chocolate—chopped
- White chocolate—chopped
- Roasted nuts: pecans, almonds, walnuts, or hazelnuts—chopped

notes and tips

- To toast nuts, place them in a 9-inch square baking pan and roast in a 325°F oven, stirring once or twice, until fragrant and slightly deeper in color, 7 to 12 minutes, depending on the size of the nuts.

- This thick batter does not spread, so you can fill or even overfill the muffin cups. ➤

pam's fave combos for big beautiful bran muffins

Cherries and bittersweet chocolate

Cranberries and white chocolate

Blueberries and cardamom

Golden raisins and cinnamon

Mixed berries and orange zest

part 2
fun food
the rest of
the day

Why divide *Cook without a Book: Meatless Meals* into only two sections, Not Strictly Breakfast and Fun Food the Rest of the Day? Aren't there at least three meals to account for in a day? Here's what I've discovered. Take meat out of the day's equation and you eat a little differently.

With meat always on the dinner menu, hearty soups, satisfying salads, and fun sandwiches often get slotted into lunch. On a meatless day you get to enjoy them for lunch or dinner. Meatless BLTs, Eat-Your-Plate Taco Salad, Chopped Egg Caesar with Hash Brown Croutons, and French Onion Soup will make you smile at either meal.

When the traditional meat, starch, and vegetable plate isn't an option, dinner might mean a quick soup bar. While the soup broth simmers with aromatics (it starts with good store-bought vegetable broth, so it doesn't take long), set out a colorful array of ingredients and toppings and let everyone have fun building his or her own Asian noodle or tortilla soup.

Meatless Mexican is fun too. Cook up a pot of Chili Lentils for a first-rate taco spread you can have on the table in under a half hour. Stuff flour tortillas with highly seasoned good-for-you fillings, and quesadillas suddenly shift from appetizer to dinner. Both of these may well become regulars on your meatless nights. Potatoes play a big part in a meatless life. Super-Fast Twice Baked Potatoes are delicious and doable on a weeknight. Choose from one of the

Spud Sauces—Mushroom-Cream with Mustard and Tarragon, Spinach-Feta with Scallions and Dill. Or go Indian with Samosa Spud Sauce. There's meatless hash too—and you don't even need leftovers to pull it off.

With a little store-bought pie dough, puff pastry, or simple baguette, I've found a way to make savory vegetable pot pies, galettes, quiches, and stratas easy weeknight standbys.

All your favorites are here too—pastas, pizzas, risottos, stir-fries, and other Asian favorites like fried rice, lo mein, and pad Thai. There's enough here to keep you cooking and eating meatless for a long, enjoyable time.

hearty
salads

In this section you'll find several kinds of salads: formulas for satisfying meatless main course salads featuring grains, legumes, and plenty of vegetables; superb meatless versions of classic favorites; and familiar side or first-course salads gone main course. Whichever way you go, there are lots of fun, satisfying options to choose from here.

meatless main course salads

Most of us don't need salad *recipes* as much as we need salad *ideas*. Without a reminder of all the amazing salad ingredients in our pantry, refrigerator, and freezer, we tend to fall into hopeless ruts. So this section is a reminder of all the satisfying, innovative salads you could make if you just took a fresh look at all those overlooked ingredients in your kitchen.

If making vinaigrette feels like one step too many, simply dress it lightly with olive oil and salt and pepper to taste, then drizzle in a little vinegar or lemon juice—go light here, knowing you can always add more. Tossed this way, your substantial main course salad could be on the table in the time it takes to make plain old tossed salad.

master formula meatless main course salad

8 cups packed Salad Greens (Pick 1 or more)
Salad Options (Pick 3 to 5)
¼ cup extra-virgin olive oil, salt and ground black pepper, 2 tablespoons Vinegar/Acid *or* ⅓ cup Dressing (Pick 1)

Place Salad Greens and Salad Ingredients in a large bowl. Drizzle with the oil and add a generous sprinkling of salt and several grinds of black pepper. Using spring-action tongs (or clean hands), toss the salad to coat evenly. Drizzle in Vinegar/Acid of choice, toss again to coat. Taste the salad and adjust the flavorings, including more vinegar (or acid), salt, or pepper. Or toss with ⅓ cup Dressing. Serve.

Serves 4

salad options

Salad Greens (Pick 1 or more)

Spring mix, arugula, baby spinach, mâche, watercress—Unless from a farmers' market, these greens usually come conveniently factory washed. If so, just dump and toss. If not, rinse and spin dry. Baby spinach is mild, as is mâche. Spring mix varies but usually contains a mix of mild and assertive greens. Mildly bitter arugula and pleasantly peppery watercress are the most distinct. Be careful not to overburden these delicate greens. Much like an overtopped thin pizza, they will collapse if overdressed or overflavored.

Hearts of romaine—Nice on their own or in combination with baby lettuces. Halve lengthwise, core, and slash each half lengthwise and crosswise for a coarse chop.

Butter lettuces (e.g., Boston or Bibb)—Mild and delicate, these lettuces don't usually pair well with heavy, bold ingredients: Roasted eggplant and Boston, for example, are not an ideal match. Think chopped boiled eggs, small white beans, mushrooms, scallions, thinly sliced radishes, and carrots. Leave smaller inner leaves whole, tear outer leaves into big pieces.

Escarole, radicchio, and Belgian endive—Because these lettuces are sturdy and assertive, make sure your salad is equally assertive (red onion, blue cheese, toasted walnuts, roasted veggies). Or use them in combination with other greens. Halve and core the radicchio, then tear it into bite-size pieces. Halve the Belgian endive, remove the core, and then slice it crosswise. Cut escarole as you would a romaine heart.

Cabbage (green, red, napa)—Cabbage adds mild pleasant crunch (and, if using red, color as well). I'm especially fond of napa cabbage, a bit of a lettuce/cabbage hybrid. To shred cabbage by hand, quarter and then core it. Separate the cabbage quarters into stacks of leaves that flatten when pressed lightly and then shred finely by hand. You can also use your food processor with the slicing disk.

Salad Options (Pick 3 to 5)

Protein

Canned beans—Black, cannellini, Great Northern, navy, chickpeas, pinto, and kidney beans. Simply drain. Rinse if you like, but I rather like the seasoned cooking liquid that adheres to the drained beans. Figure about one 16-ounce can, drained. You can also use 1½ cups of cooked lentils (page 269).

Nuts and seeds—Almonds, cashews, pecans, walnuts, hazelnuts, pistachios, peanuts, pine nuts, candied nuts, pumpkin or sunflower seeds. Buy them already roasted if you can, or follow roasting instructions on page 270. Figure ¼ cup.

Cheeses—Stick with more assertive cheeses: aged or extra-sharp Cheddar; crumbled goat, blue, feta, ricotta salata, and queso fresco; shaved or grated Parmesan cheese. Smoked cheese (gouda, Cheddar, mozzarella, Gruyère) coupled with crunch (pita chips, melba toast, or bagel crisps) does a pretty good bacon impression. Figure about 4 ounces.

Boiled eggs—Even in my more carnivorous days I nearly always had a bowl of boiled eggs marked with an X in the fridge. These days, they're essential. Figure 3 to 4.

Tofu—Baked tofu comes seasoned in many varieties; slice or cube an 8-ounce package.

Fruits

Fresh—Depending on the season, consider the following: sliced apples, strawberries, peaches, plums, apricots, and pears; quartered figs; halved grapes; sectioned oranges, grapefruits; chunks of mango, pineapple, and melon; summer berries (blackberries, blueberries, raspberries); and pomegranate seeds. Figure about 2 cups.

Dried—Cranberries, cherries, blueberries, raisins (golden and dark); chopped apricots, pears, peaches, prunes, figs, and dates. Figure about ½ cup.

Vegetables

Raw—Tomatoes, bell peppers, carrots, celery, corn kernels cut from the cob, cucumbers, red onions, radishes, scallions, mushrooms, avocado (technically fruit, but really . . .), fennel, and bean sprouts. For me, red onions or scallions are always part of the mix. Figure about 2 cups total.

Cooked—Any roasted vegetable: potatoes, sweet potatoes, carrots, beets, parsnips, turnips (white or yellow), asparagus, onions, eggplant, zucchini, fennel, mushrooms, cauliflower, cherry tomatoes; or steamed broccoli. Figure about 2 cups total. (See page 270 for cooking guidelines.)

Frozen—Corn, lima beans, edamame, and green peas. Steam or microwave to a hot state and then cool slightly before adding to the salad. Figure about 1½ cups.

Pantry Items

Capers, olives of all kinds, sun-dried tomatoes, roasted red peppers, cornichons (figure about ½ cup of these), artichoke hearts, water chestnuts (about 1 cup of these).

Crunchy Things

Good-quality croutons, crumbled melba toast, pita chips, bagel crisps, tortilla chips, oyster crackers, Chinese noodles. Figure 1 cup.

Herbs

Chopped soft fresh ones like dill, basil, tarragon, cilantro, parsley, mint, or oregano. Figure ¼ cup, but you may want more of basil, cilantro, and parsley.

Vinegar/Acids

Balsamic and rice vinegars are better with sweet salads; sherry and red wine vinegars tend to work better with savory salads; lemon or lime juice can usually go either way.

Dressings

With such flavorful ingredients, all you really need to complete the salad is the light drizzle of oil and vinegar suggested in the Master Formula. But if you want to add a little something extra, try one of these options.

Select one based on the types of ingredients to be dressed (sturdy lettuces like romaine stand up to heavier dressings like Caesar) or the predominant acid.

- **Light Blue Cheese Dressing (page 94)**
- **Creamy Salsa Dressing (page 103)**
- **Caesar Dressing (page 99)**
- **Sherry Vinaigrette (page 105)**
- **Balsamic Vinaigrette (page 104)**
- **Sweet Ginger Dressing (page 100)**
- **Lemon-Feta-Dill Vinaigrette (page 93)**
- **Lemon-Mustard Vinaigrette (page 97)**

pam's fave combos for meatless main course salads

Escarole, white beans, feta, red onion, and roasted red pepper

Spring mix, fresh fruit in season, goat cheese, red onion, candied nuts

Arugula, chickpeas, pistachios, red onion, dried apricots, pita chips

Romaine hearts, black beans, corn, scallions, queso fresco, crumbled toasted tortillas

Baby spinach, beets, boiled eggs, red onion, ricotta salata

Mixed greens, mushrooms, boiled eggs, green peas, fennel, scallions

Romaine hearts, baked tofu, celery, Parmesan, pimiento-stuffed olives, melba toast

notes and tips

• These days salad greens tend to come in 5-, 7-, or 16-ounce containers that make it easy to eyeball the amount of salad greens you may need. If you buy loose greens or a much larger container, you can get a relatively accurate measurement without weighing them by stuffing the greens in one of those 1-quart plastic deli containers. One packed container is about 4 cups, or enough for 2 main course salads; 2 filled containers is enough for 4.

• To dress the salad simply, drizzle on oil and season with salt and pepper; toss to coat evenly with the oil. Add a squirt of lemon juice or other acid; toss to coat again. Taste and adjust seasoning to your liking. ➤

grain and legume salads

Since legumes—peas, beans, lentils, edamame, and peanuts—coupled with either nuts or grains form a complete protein, the hearty main course grain and legume salads in this chapter can be a vibrant, satisfying way to get meatless protein into your diet—and vegetables too!

I offer 10 very different grain and legume salads—so different, in fact, it's hard to believe they derive from the same formula, but they do. The formula is simple. For 4 main course servings you need 4 cups total of legumes and/or grains.

If you've got time, bulk up your salad with cooked vegetables—broiled zucchini, cooked sweet potatoes, steamed broccoli or asparagus, for example. And here's the place to tailor the salad to the season—green beans and tomatoes for a summer grain and legume salad, sweet potatoes or winter squash and broccoli in the cooler months, asparagus, carrots, and green peas for spring.

Extra ingredients add depth, texture, and personality—nuts, dried fruit, cheeses, and pantry items all work here. Grain and legume salads need a little onion too—any will do—but I prefer the touch of color red onions or scallions bring to the mix. With such a flavorful salad, you could leave out the fresh herbs, but I like the way they further perk up the salad's flavor and color.

master formula grain and legume salads

4 cups Cooked Grains and/or Legumes (Pick 1 or 2)

3 cups Raw and/or Cooked Vegetables (Pick 1 or 2 cooked and/or 2 or 3 raw)

$\frac{1}{2}$ cup Extras (Pick 1 or 2; optional)

$\frac{1}{4}$ medium onion or 4 scallions, thinly sliced (about $\frac{1}{2}$ cup)

$\frac{1}{4}$ cup chopped fresh herbs (parsley, cilantro, basil, mint, or a mix)

$\frac{1}{3}$ cup Dressing (Pick 1) *or* **$\frac{1}{4}$ cup extra-virgin olive oil, salt and pepper, and 2 tablespoons vinegar**

Prepare the Cooked Grains and/or Legumes; place in a large bowl.

Meanwhile, prepare the Raw and/or Cooked Vegetables; add to the bowl.

Prepare the Extra(s) if using, slice onions, and chop herbs; add to bowl.

If making Dressing, do it now. When ready to serve, add dressing to salad ingredients; toss to coat. Or, drizzle salad with olive oil and sprinkle with salt and pepper to taste; toss to coat. Add vinegar; toss to coat again. Adjust seasonings and serve.

Serves 4

salad options

Cooked Grains and/or Legumes* (Pick 1 or 2; you'll need 4 cups total)

Grains

- Rice (brown or white)
- Quinoa (red, white, or a mix)
- Barley
- Bulgur
- Pasta, bite-size (whole-grain or regular)
- Couscous, regular or Israeli
- Millet
- Wheatberries, farro, or spelt

Legumes

- Lentils
- Beans, canned or cooked: chickpeas, white beans (Great Northern, navy, cannellini), black beans, pinto beans, kidney beans (dark or light), black-eyed peas

Raw and/or Cooked Vegetables* (Pick 2 or 3 raw and/or 1 or 2 cooked; you'll need 3 cups total)

Raw or Thawed Frozen Vegetables (Pick 2 or 3)

- **Carrots**—Peeled and coarsely grated or thinly sliced
- **Celery**—Finely diced
- **Hothouse (seedless) cucumbers**—Partially peeled (I like to leave a few strips of peel for color), cut into small dice, and lightly salted
- **Cherry or grape tomatoes**—Halved if small, quartered if large; lightly salted
- **Bell peppers**—Stemmed, cored, and finely diced
- **Cabbage**—Quartered, cored, separated into stacks that flatten when pressed lightly, and shredded finely by hand or using the food processor slicing disk
- **Fennel**—Stalks discarded, cored, and thinly sliced
- **Lima beans, corn, edamame, green peas**— A 10-ounce package is about 2 cups. Thaw for 3 to 4 minutes in the microwave.
- **Artichoke hearts**—Use a 9-ounce package frozen (thawed) or a 14-ounce can (drained). The yield on both is about 2 cups.

Cooked Vegetables (Pick 1 or 2)

- **Broiled asparagus**—A 1-pound bunch, trimmed and cooked, should yield a generous 2 cups.
- **Steamed broccoli and cauliflower florets**
- **Broiled zucchini and yellow squash**
- **Steamed or roasted root vegetables (turnips, rutabagas, parsnips, and potatoes) and winter squash**

See the appendix beginning on page 268 for notes on cooking grains, legumes, and vegetables.

Optional Extras (Pick 1 or 2; you'll need $^1/_2$ cup total)

Nuts and seeds—Toasted or roasted almonds (slivered or sliced); coarsely chopped pecans, walnuts, hazelnuts, or cashews; pistachios, pine nuts, or hulled pumpkin seeds.

Dried fruit—Cranberries, cherries, or raisins (golden or dark); chopped apricots, peaches, or dates.

Cheeses—Crumbled feta, goat, blue; coarsely grated or shaved Parmesan cheese.

Pantry items—Chopped sun-dried tomatoes, olives (black, Kalamata, pimiento-stuffed), or roasted red peppers.

Dressings (Pick 1)

- **Sherry Vinaigrette (page 105)**
- **Balsamic Vinaigrette (page 104)**
- **Lemon-Mustard Vinaigrette (page 97)**
- **Lime Vinaigrette:** Follow the recipe for Lemon-Mustard Vinaigrette, substituting an equal amount of lime juice for the lemon juice
- **Red Wine Vinaigrette:** Follow the recipe for Lemon-Mustard Vinaigrette, substituting an equal amount of red wine vinegar for the lemon juice

notes and tips

- Unlike instant brown rice, which actually has a little character, instant white rice is mushy. I don't recommend it.

- Since you'll probably already be cooking a grain, you'll likely rely on canned beans. Unfortunately a 15- to 16-ounce can is only about $1^1/_2$ cups of drained beans. To get the 2 cups you need you have 2 choices—open 2 cans and use the leftovers in soups, salads, quesadillas, pastas etc., or open just 1 can and compensate with extra grains.

- If you're looking for really fast food, mix 3 scant cans of drained beans in a bowl with a couple of the suggested raw vegetables, add a flavoring or two, toss with oil and vinegar, and you're ready to serve up.

- For a complete-protein meal, even a mix of legumes and grains can be simple. Cooked plain brown and white rice are available at just about any grocery store, and there's quick-cooking pasta, which is done in about 3 minutes. For DIY grains, however, I offer multiple cooking methods for most of the major ones on page 268.

pam's fave combos for grain and/or legume salads

Couscous and Chickpea Salad with Zucchini, Raisins, and Pine Nuts: 2 cups cooked couscous (Israeli or regular), 2 cups drained canned chickpeas, 3 cups broiled sliced zucchini, ¼ cup golden raisins, ¼ cup toasted pine nuts,* ¼ cup chopped fresh cilantro, ⅓ cup Balsamic Vinaigrette (page 104); or dress with olive oil and balsamic vinegar

Quinoa and Black Bean Salad with Tomatoes and Cucumbers: 2 cups cooked quinoa, 2 cups canned black beans, 1½ cups *each* grape or cherry tomatoes (lightly salted), 1½ cups finely diced cucumber (lightly salted), ½ cup toasted pumpkin or sunflower seeds (or ½ cup queso fresco), ¼ cup chopped fresh cilantro, ⅓ cup Lime Vinaigrette (page 88); or dress with olive oil and lime juice

To quickly toast pine nuts, cook them in a small skillet over medium-low heat, shaking the skillet occasionally, until light golden brown, about 5 minutes. Transfer to a plate to cool.

Orzo and White Bean Salad with Asparagus, Artichokes, Almonds, and Parsley: 2 cups *each* cooked orzo and drained canned white beans, 1½ cups *each* artichoke hearts and broiled asparagus pieces, ¼ cup each toasted sliced or slivered almonds and grated Parmesan cheese, ¼ cup chopped fresh parsley, ⅓ cup Lemon-Mustard Vinaigrette (page 97); or dress with olive oil and lemon juice

Bulgur Wheat and Lima Bean Salad with Tabouleh Flavorings: 2 cups *each* cooked bulgur wheat and thawed frozen lima beans, 1½ cups *each* halved grape or cherry tomatoes and small-diced cucumber, lightly salted, ½ cup coarsely chopped pimiento-stuffed olives, 2 tablespoons *each* chopped fresh parsley and mint (feel free to increase the parsley and/or mint on this one), ⅓ cup Lemon-Mustard Vinaigrette (page 97); or dress with olive oil and lemon juice

Sweet Potato and Brown Rice Salad with Pistachios and Dried Cherries: 4 cups cooked brown rice, 3 cups cooked sweet potatoes, ¼ cup *each* coarsely chopped roasted pistachios and dried cherries, ¼ cup chopped fresh cilantro, ⅓ cup Balsamic Vinaigrette (page 104); or dress with olive oil and balsamic vinegar. Season this salad to your taste with a little curry powder if you like.

Pasta and White Bean Salad with Broccoli, Pine Nuts, and Sun-Dried Tomatoes: 2 cups *each* cooked bow-tie (or other bite-size) pasta and drained canned navy beans, 3 cups steamed broccoli florets and sliced stems, ¼ cup *each* toasted pine nuts and finely chopped sun-dried tomatoes, ¼ cup chopped fresh basil, ⅓ cup Lemon-Mustard Vinaigrette (page 97); or dress with olive oil and lemon juice

Barley and Lentil Salad with Mushrooms, Walnut, Cranberries, and Thyme: 2 cups *each* cooked barley and lentils, 3 cups sautéed mushrooms, ¼ cup each dried cranberries and coarsely chopped roasted walnuts, Balsamic Vinaigrette (page 104); or dress with olive oil and balsamic vinegar. Here's a slight variation on the herb theme. Instead of using ¼ cup soft, mild herbs, I'm using 1 tablespoon thyme, a more assertive fresh herb, along with 3 tablespoons parsley for a total of ¼ cup. This 1:3 ratio would also work with dill and tarragon.

Wheatberry and Corn with Green Beans, Tomatoes, and Almonds: 2 cups *each* cooked wheatberries and corn, 1½ cups *each* halved cherry tomatoes (lightly salted) and cooked green beans, ¼ cup chopped fresh basil leaves, ⅓ cup Lemon-Mustard Vinaigrette (page 97); or dress with olive oil and lemon juice

Orecchiette and White Bean with Cauliflower, Pimiento-Stuffed Olives, and Almonds: 2 cups *each* cooked orecchiette and drained canned cannellini beans, 3 cups cooked cauliflower, ¼ cup *each* toasted sliced or slivered almonds and coarsely chopped pimiento-stuffed olives, 2 tablespoons *each* chopped fresh basil and parsley, Red Wine Vinaigrette (page 88); or dress with olive oil and red wine vinegar

Brown Rice and Black-Eyed Peas with Carrots, Bell Pepper, and Sun-Dried Tomatoes: 2 cups *each* cooked brown rice and drained canned black-eyed peas, 2 cups (2 large) peeled and grated carrots, ½ cup *each* diced celery and yellow bell pepper, ¼ cup *each* coarsely chopped sun-dried tomatoes and crumbled goat cheese, ¼ cup chopped fresh parsley, Sherry or Red Wine Vinaigrette (pages 105 and 88); or dress with olive oil and sherry or red wine vinegar

classic salads made meatless

The recipes that follow aren't formulas, but they are each worthy additions to your salad repertoire, all adapted to the meatless table.

In Meatless Cobb (page 94), smoked mozzarella coupled with crumbled pita chips take the place of crisp smoky bacon and mild chopped chicken, while grilled corn on the cob makes a fun stand-in for the usual chicken or flank steak in Eat-Your-Plate Taco Salad with Black Beans and Grilled Corn (page 103). With this salad or any of the others in this chapter, bake your own edible flour tortilla plates. (They're ready in just 8 minutes.)

Tuna Niçoise is always a lovely warm-weather salad. Swap artichokes for fish and drizzle the composed salad with chunky feta-dill vinaigrette, and you've got a beautiful Tuna-less Niçoise. And while there is no real substitute for bacon, Parmigiano-Reggiano shavings turn Spinach Salad with Mushrooms and Chopped Egg (page 97) into a satisfying main course.

Not only does chopped egg make Caesar salad (page 99) more substantial, it pairs perfectly with the creamy lemon dressing; and sautéed hash browns (rather than the usual bread) make a fun crouton. Potato salad is always an appealing side dish. Add mashed tofu to the mix and serve it on a bed of greens for a satisfying meal. Beet salad with goat cheese and walnuts is always a great start to a meal. Toss in a can of kidney beans and suddenly it's dinner.

Pair classic Waldorf ingredients—apples, celery, and walnuts—with golden raisins, blue cheese, and napa cabbage for a salad that will stick with you. And finally, if you're looking for an excuse to enjoy an egg roll, fry some up and serve them on a bed of napa cabbage slaw tossed with a sweet ginger dressing. After all, as we know, there are no calories in a salad!

tuna-less niçoise with lemon-feta-dill vinaigrette

You won't be missing the tuna in this highly flavored, meatless take on the classic Niçoise. Make a dill vinaigrette, sub artichoke hearts and potatoes for tuna, and heighten the flavor with a little feta.

Lemon-Feta-Dill Vinaigrette
2 tablespoons Dijon mustard
2 tablespoons fresh lemon juice
1 tablespoon rice vinegar
1 large shallot, minced
3 tablespoons chopped fresh dill leaves
Salt and ground black pepper
$\frac{1}{2}$ cup extra-virgin olive oil
$\frac{1}{2}$ cup crumbled feta cheese

Salad
1 pound small red potatoes, thickly sliced
1 tablespoon plus 2 teaspoons olive oil
Salt and ground black pepper
$\frac{3}{4}$ pound green beans, trimmed
1 cup drained marinated artichoke hearts
2 medium tomatoes, cut into thin wedges
  and lightly salted
4 hard-boiled eggs (see page 172), quartered
$\frac{1}{2}$ cup pitted piquant black olives, such as
  Kalamata or Niçoise

To make the vinaigrette: Whisk the mustard, lemon juice, vinegar, shallot, dill, a big pinch of salt, and a few grinds of pepper in a small bowl or 2-cup glass measuring cup. Slowly whisk in the oil, first in droplets and then in a steady stream, to make a thick vinaigrette. Whisk in the feta and set aside.

To make the salad: Toss the potatoes with 1 tablespoon of the oil and a sprinkling of salt and pepper. Spread out on a rimmed baking sheet in a single layer. Set the pan on the lowest rack in a cold oven. Turn the oven to 450°F and roast the potatoes until the bottoms are impressively brown, about 20 minutes. Turn the potatoes over and roast until the second side is browned, about 5 minutes longer. Let cool slightly.

Meanwhile, place the beans, $\frac{1}{3}$ cup of water, the remaining 2 teaspoons oil, and $\frac{1}{4}$ teaspoon salt in a medium (10-inch) skillet. Cover the skillet, set over high heat, and cook until the water has mostly evaporated and the beans are bright and just tender, 5 to 7 minutes. Spread onto a rimmed baking sheet to stop the cooking.

When ready to serve, arrange the potatoes, beans, artichoke hearts, tomato wedges, and eggs on each of 4 dinner plates. Scatter the olives over the arranged salad and drizzle with a little vinaigrette. Serve with extra vinaigrette passed separately.

Serves 4

meatless cobb

If you need egg-boiling instructions, see page 172. You will probably use only about half the dressing for this salad. Use it for topping other salads later in the week or as a dip for crudités.

Light Blue Cheese Dressing
$\frac{1}{3}$ cup buttermilk
$\frac{1}{3}$ cup reduced-fat sour cream
$\frac{1}{3}$ cup low-fat mayonnaise
1 teaspoon red wine vinegar
$\frac{1}{2}$ teaspoon garlic powder
$\frac{1}{4}$ teaspoon vegetarian Worcestershire sauce
$\frac{1}{2}$ cup crumbled blue cheese
Salt and ground black pepper to taste

Salad
8 lightly packed cups (about 8 ounces) prewashed mixed baby greens
4 ounces smoked mozzarella, cut into small dice
4 hard-boiled eggs, peeled and cut into small dice
2 small tomatoes, cut into small dice
1 Hass avocado, cut into small dice
$\frac{1}{2}$ small red onion, cut into small dice
1 cup coarsely crumbled pita chips

To make the dressing: Stir together all dressing ingredients, mashing some of the blue cheese into the dressing with the back of a fork. (The dressing can be covered and refrigerated for several days.)

To assemble the salad: Place the salad greens in a large bowl. Arrange the mozzarella, eggs, tomatoes, avocado, and onion in strips over the salad greens. (The composed salad can be covered and refrigerated several hours ahead.)

When ready to serve, drizzle the salad with dressing to taste and sprinkle with the pita chips. Toss and serve immediately.

Serves 4

- To easily cube avocado, score the flesh lengthwise and crosswise and scoop out with a spoon. ➤

- To more evenly distribute the blue cheese, use a fork to mash some of it into the dressing. ➤

waldorf slaw with blue cheese and honey

If you are tempted to leave out the honey, don't. You don't need much and it's the ingredient that really pulls the salad together.

4 cups (about ½ medium head) shredded napa cabbage
1 large or 2 small crisp apples, quartered and thinly sliced crosswise
2 large celery ribs, cut into medium dice
½ cup dried cranberries or golden raisins
½ cup toasted walnuts, chopped
4 ounces crumbled blue cheese
¼ cup extra-virgin olive oil
Salt and ground black pepper
4 teaspoons rice vinegar
4 teaspoons honey

Combine the cabbage, apple(s), celery, cranberries, walnuts, and blue cheese in a large bowl. Drizzle with the oil and sprinkle with salt and pepper to taste. Toss to coat. Drizzle in the vinegar and honey, toss well to coat again, and serve.

Serves 4

spinach salad with mushrooms & chopped egg

Use a vegetable peeler to shave thin cheese curls from a block of Reggiano. For a little crunch, crumble in a couple of handfuls of plain pita chips or melba toasts. You can also toss the salad with Balsamic Vinaigrette (page 104).

Lemon-Mustard Vinaigrette
1 medium garlic clove, minced
2 tablespoons fresh lemon juice
2 tablespoons Dijon mustard
1 tablespoon rice vinegar
Salt and ground black pepper
$\frac{1}{2}$ cup extra-virgin olive oil

Salad
8 ounces sliced mushrooms
$1\frac{1}{2}$ tablespoons olive oil
Salt and ground black pepper
8 cups (about 8 ounces) prewashed baby spinach
3 hard-boiled eggs, chopped
$\frac{1}{2}$ medium red onion, thinly sliced
1 cup shaved Parmigiano-Reggiano cheese

To make the vinaigrette: Whisk the garlic, lemon juice, mustard, vinegar, a big pinch of salt, and a few grinds of pepper in a small bowl or 2-cup glass measuring cup. Slowly whisk in the oil, first in droplets and then in a steady stream, to make a thick vinaigrette.

To assemble the salad: A few minutes before serving, toss the mushrooms in a medium bowl with the oil and a light sprinkling of salt and pepper. Place the spinach in a large bowl. Add the mushrooms, eggs, and red onion and about $\frac{1}{4}$ cup of dressing; toss to coat. Add $\frac{3}{4}$ cup of the Parmesan and additional dressing, if needed to coat; toss again. Serve, sprinkling each salad with some of the remaining $\frac{1}{4}$ cup of cheese shavings.

Serves 4

chopped egg caesar with hash brown croutons

Squares of hash brown patties provide a heartier crouton than the standard bread variety, but crisping the small squares requires patience and a good set of spring-action tongs. If you want to keep it simple, just heat the oil (you'll need 2 tablespoons instead of 1) in the skillet and fry the patties whole, cutting them into squares once they've crisped up.

Caesar Dressing

2 tablespoons fresh lemon juice
2½ tablespoons mayonnaise, light or regular
1 medium garlic clove, sliced, smashed with the flat blade of a knife, then minced to a paste
¼ teaspoon vegetarian Worcestershire sauce
Salt and ground black pepper
5 tablespoons pure olive oil
¼ cup finely grated Parmesan cheese

Croutons and Salad

4 frozen hash brown patties, unthawed, cut into 1-inch squares (see above)
1 generous tablespoon olive oil
3 large romaine hearts, halved lengthwise, cored, and chopped (about 8 cups)
3 hard-boiled eggs, chopped
¼ cup coarsely grated Parmesan cheese, plus more for sprinkling

To make the dressing: Whisk the lemon juice, mayonnaise, garlic, Worcestershire sauce, a pinch of salt, and a few grinds of pepper in a small bowl. Slowly whisk in the oil to make a creamy dressing. Stir in the Parmesan.

To make the croutons: Heat a 12-inch skillet over medium heat. Place the frozen hash brown squares in a medium bowl, drizzle with the oil, and toss to coat. Add the hash browns to the hot skillet and cook, turning the cubes only once, until crisp and golden brown, about 10 minutes. Remove from the heat and let the hash browns stand uncovered until ready to assemble the salad.

To assemble the salad: Place the lettuce and eggs in a large bowl. Add the dressing and toss to coat. Add the hash browns and toss again. Add the Parmesan and toss once more. Serve immediately, sprinkling each salad with a little more Parmesan cheese if you'd like.

Serves 4

◄ Use a Microplane grater, if you've got one, to grate the cheese that gets stirred into the dressing. Switch to a coarse grater or even a vegetable peeler for the cheese that's sprinkled over the finished salad.

◄ Slicing the garlic into coins before smashing ensures a fine mince.

vegetable egg rolls on napa-carrot salad

If you don't have time to make the egg rolls, simply pick up vegetable egg rolls at your local Chinese restaurant (ask for partially fried egg rolls that have not been given a second dip in the fryer to reheat) and follow instructions in Quick Vegetable Egg Rolls for a final flash fry. Or pick up good-quality frozen vegetable egg rolls. If using frozen, use the package instructions as a guide, but I generally find they need to be fried at a lower temperature than what is called for and for a little longer: 6 to 7 minutes at about 350°F usually gets them very crisp and impressively brown.

Sweet Ginger Dressing
¼ cup pure olive oil
2 tablespoons honey
2 tablespoons rice vinegar
2 tablespoons soy sauce
2 teaspoons minced garlic
2 teaspoons minced fresh ginger
¼ teaspoon red pepper flakes

Salad
4 cups (about ½ medium head) shredded
  napa cabbage
2 large carrots, peeled and grated
2 large scallions, thinly sliced
Quick Vegetable Egg Rolls (recipe follows),
  freshly fried

To make the dressing: Combine the oil, honey, vinegar, soy sauce, 1 tablespoon water, garlic, ginger, and red pepper flakes in a lidded jar. Shake to combine.

To assemble the salad: Combine the cabbage, carrots, and scallions in a medium bowl. Add 6 tablespoons of the dressing and toss to coat. Place a portion of slaw on each of 4 salad plates. Top each salad with 4 egg roll halves and serve immediately with extra dressing passed separately.

Serves 4

quick vegetable egg rolls

Makes 8 egg rolls (but doubles easily)

1 tablespoon vegetable oil, plus 2 cups for frying
1 package (8 ounces) coleslaw mix
Salt
¼ cup sliced scallions
1 tablespoon creamy peanut butter
8 egg roll wrappers
2 tablespoons minced fresh cilantro

Heat 1 tablespoon of the oil in a medium (10-inch) skillet until it starts to shimmer and wisps of smoke are just visible. Add the coleslaw mix, season lightly with salt, and cook until just wilted, 1 to 2 minutes. Transfer the mixture to a medium bowl and stir in the scallions and peanut butter until evenly distributed.

Place an egg roll wrapper on a work surface. Place 2 tablespoons of the filling just below the center, forming it into a log. Fold both sides of the wrapper in over filling. Starting at the end closer to you, fold the wrapper over the filling, then roll it as tightly as you can. Moisten the wrapper end with wet fingertips and press it to the roll to seal. Repeat with remaining filling and wrappers.

The par-cooked egg rolls can be cooked, wrapped, and refrigerated for up to 3 days.

Heat the remaining 2 cups oil in a Dutch oven or small soup kettle to 300°F. Cook the egg rolls 4 at a time, turning once, until fried through but still blond, about 2 minutes. Drain on a wire rack.

When ready to serve, reheat the oil to 375°F. Cook the egg rolls 4 at a time, turning once, until crisp and golden brown, about 2 minutes. Return to the wire rack to drain briefly. Halve each roll on the diagonal, dipping each cut end in cilantro.

eat-your-plate taco salad with black beans and grilled corn

If you like, sprinkle the tossed salad with a little chopped fresh cilantro.

2½ tablespoons olive oil
4 flour tortillas (8-inch), pricked all over with a fork
Kosher salt
1 tablespoon garlic powder
1 tablespoon ground cumin
1 tablespoon dried oregano
4 ears of corn, shucked and halved crosswise
2 to 3 romaine hearts, halved lengthwise, cored, and coarsely chopped (8 cups)
1 cup grape or cherry tomatoes, halved and lightly salted
1 yellow bell pepper, stemmed, cored, and cut into short, thin strips
4 scallions, thinly sliced (about ½ cup)
1 can (15.5 ounces) black beans, drained
1 cup grated pepper Jack cheese (about 4 ounces)

Creamy Salsa Dressing
½ cup reduced-fat sour cream, plus extra for garnish
½ cup prepared salsa verde or tomato salsa, plus extra for serving

Adjust the oven rack to the middle position and preheat the oven to 350°F. Use 1½ tablespoons of the oil to lightly brush both sides of the tortillas; sprinkle them with salt. Arrange directly on the oven rack and bake, turning once, until crisp and golden brown, about 5 minutes on the first side and 3 minutes on the second side (use the tip of a knife to deflate any air pockets that may balloon during baking); set aside.

Mix the remaining 1 tablespoon oil with the garlic powder, cumin, and oregano and rub onto the corn to evenly coat. Sprinkle generously with salt.

Meanwhile preheat a gas grill with all burners on high for about 10 minutes. Use a wire brush to clean the grill rack, then use tongs to wipe a vegetable oil–soaked rag over it. Close the lid and return to temperature. When very hot, place the corn on the hot rack; cover and grill, turning as needed, until spotted with brown, about 10 minutes.

Combine the lettuce, tomatoes, bell pepper, scallions, black beans, and cheese in a large bowl. To make the dressing, stir together the sour cream and salsa. Add half the dressing to the salad and toss to coat. Heap a portion of salad onto each flour tortilla. Serve with ears of corn alongside. Garnish if you like with a little extra sour cream and serve with additional dressing alongside.

Serves 4

beet and kidney bean salad with goat cheese and walnuts

Choose a bunch of beets with bright, fresh, unbruised greens for this. If you don't want to fire up the oven, a toaster oven is the ideal appliance for roasting the beets. While they cool, reduce the temperature to 325°F and toast the walnuts for 10 minutes, until fragrant. Fortunately there will be leftover vinaigrette to dress other salads throughout the week.

Balsamic Vinaigrette

1 large garlic clove, minced
$\frac{1}{3}$ cup balsamic vinegar
2 tablespoons Dijon mustard
$\frac{1}{4}$ teaspoon salt
$\frac{1}{4}$ teaspoon ground black pepper
Generous $\frac{1}{2}$ cup extra-virgin olive oil

Salad

1 bunch beets (4 medium) with greens
1 can (15 to 16 ounces) dark kidney beans, drained
$\frac{1}{2}$ small red onion, thinly sliced
4 ounces crumbled goat cheese
$\frac{1}{4}$ cup chopped toasted walnuts (see above or page 270 for toasting instructions)

To make the vinaigrette: Whisk the garlic, vinegar, mustard, salt, and pepper in a 2-cup glass measuring cup. Slowly whisk in the oil until you reach the 1-cup mark; set aside.

To assemble the salad: Adjust the oven rack to the middle position and preheat the oven to 400°F. Trim the greens from the beets. Wash the beets and wrap individually in foil. Place the beets in a small baking pan and roast until a thin blade can be inserted easily, 45 minutes to 1 hour.

Meanwhile, stem, wash, dry, and finely shred the beet greens.

When the beets are cool enough to handle, peel (the skins slip right off), slice, and place in a medium bowl. Add the beans, onion, and 3 tablespoons of the vinaigrette and toss to coat.

When ready to serve, toss the beet greens with 3 tablespoons of the vinaigrette and divide among 4 plates. Top with a portion of the beet mixture and sprinkle with goat cheese and walnuts.

Serves 4

roasted potato and tofu salad

Use whatever potatoes you like, but I always try to have a sweet potato in the mix. Small potatoes are the most attractive in this salad, but if you use larger potatoes, halve them before slicing.

Sherry Vinaigrette
1 medium garlic clove, minced
3 tablespoons sherry vinegar
3 tablespoons Dijon mustard
2 tablespoons drained capers
Salt and ground black pepper
9 tablespoons extra-virgin olive oil

Salad
2 pounds small potatoes (preferably a combination of purple, Yukon Gold, red-skinned, and sweet potatoes), peeled and thickly sliced
2 tablespoons olive oil
1 teaspoon dried thyme leaves
Salt and ground black pepper
7 to 8 ounces drained extra-firm tofu ($\frac{1}{2}$ package), wrapped in a towel and pressed to remove extra liquid, and crumbled with a fork
$\frac{1}{2}$ medium red onion, thinly sliced
$\frac{1}{2}$ cup finely diced celery heart
$\frac{1}{2}$ cup pimiento-stuffed olives, chopped
4 packed cups (about 4 ounces) prewashed mixed baby greens

To make the dressing: Whisk the garlic, vinegar, mustard, capers, a big pinch of salt, and a few grinds of pepper in a small bowl or 2-cup glass measuring cup. Whisk in the oil, first in droplets and then in a steady stream, to make a thick vinaigrette.

To assemble the salad: Toss the potatoes with the oil, thyme, and a generous sprinkling of salt and pepper; spread out on a large rimmed baking sheet in a single layer. Set pan on the lowest rack in a cold oven. Turn the oven to 450°F and roast until the bottoms of the potato pieces are impressively brown, about 20 minutes. Turn the potatoes, return to the oven, and roast until the second side is browned, about 5 minutes longer. Remove from oven and let cool slightly.

Meanwhile, place the tofu, onion, celery, and olives in a large bowl.

Add the warm potatoes to the tofu mixture. Place the greens in a medium bowl and toss with 3 tablespoons of the vinaigrette. Toss the potato mixture with the remaining dressing.

When ready to serve, divide the dressed greens among 4 pasta plates and top with a portion of the potato mixture.

Serves 4

soups and skillet stews

I would happily eat soup three meals a day, and very often dinner is a bowl of soup and a hunk of hearty whole grain bread and cheese. Supper soup bars are a fun option for entertaining, as everyone helps themselves to ingredients before the hot broth is ladled on, and creamy vegetable soups are wintertime staples.

Until recently, though, I didn't think there were many soups worth eating that didn't start with a whole chicken, a ham bone, or maybe a little stewing beef. At the very least, a bit of sausage or bacon. Although I continue to make chicken noodle soup, Brunswick stew, and clam chowder, I do so with less frequency now that I understand that there is life beyond chicken broth.

But it does take some getting used to. Simply swapping vegetable broth for chicken in a favorite recipe rarely works. The fact is, vegetable broth is a little like nonalcoholic beer. It's similar, but it's missing something. Thankfully there are a number of decent vegetable broths out there—Imagine Brand, Kitchen Basics, and Pacific are some of my favorites—and if you start with a good one, perhaps boosting the flavor with white or red miso, it's not hard to make a superb meatless soup.

creamy roasted vegetable soups

I'm a big fan of smooth vegetable soups, but I always wished the flavor could be a little more robust. Then I figured out the secret: roasting. From previous experience, I knew that getting a little color on the vegetables (as opposed to just boiling them) was key to a more flavorful soup. However, sautéing the large quantity of vegetables needed for a flavorful soup in a soup pot took nearly 20 minutes and a lot of stirring and babying to get them even remotely brown.

Then I devised this much simpler—and better—method. I toss the cut vegetables with oil, salt, and pepper (and a big pinch of sugar to encourage browning) right in a roasting pan. With the oven in preheat mode, the vegetables "oven sauté" effortlessly while I prepare the rest of the soup. By the time I've chopped an onion, sliced garlic, measured herbs and/or spices, sautéed the lot, and got the broth simmering it's been 20 minutes, at which point the vegetables are beautifully browned and fully cooked. They go into the simmering broth, and in just a few minutes, the soup is ready to puree.

These soups are single-vegetable and intense, so I never make a meal out of them. Rather, they're something I enjoy alongside a salad or sandwich or at the start of a nice meal.

master formula creamy roasted vegetable soup

2 pounds Roasting Vegetables (Pick 1)
2 tablespoons olive oil
Salt and ground black pepper
1 teaspoon sugar
1 large onion, cut into large dice
3 large garlic cloves, thickly sliced
Spice Blends (Pick 1)
½ cup white wine
1 quart vegetable broth
½ cup packed cilantro or parsley leaves (optional)
1 cup evaporated milk
Garnish (optional; page 112)

Toss the Roasting Vegetable with 1 tablespoon of the oil, a generous sprinkling of salt and pepper, and the sugar. Spread out on a large rimmed baking sheet and set in a cold oven with the rack adjusted to the lowest position. Preheat the oven to 425°F. Roast the vegetables, checking on them once or twice and turning as needed to ensure even cooking, until golden brown, about 20 minutes.

Meanwhile, heat the remaining 1 tablespoon oil over medium-high heat in a soup kettle. Add the onion and cook until softened, about 5 minutes. Add the garlic and cook until fragrant, a minute or so longer.

Add the Spice Blend and roasted vegetables and cook until fragrant and the vegetables are coated, 30 seconds to a minute longer. Add the wine, simmer for a few seconds, and then add the broth. Bring to a boil, reduce to low, and simmer, partially covered, for about 5 minutes to blend the flavors.

Working in batches, transfer the vegetable mixture to a blender. Add the cilantro or parsley (if using). Puree until very smooth, 30 seconds to a minute per batch. Return to the pot and stir in the evaporated milk. Thin with water to a soupy consistency, yet thick enough to float a garnish. Heat through, ladle into small bowls, garnish if you like, and serve hot.

Makes 2 quarts, serving 8

roasted vegetable soup options

Roasting Vegetables (Pick 1)

- Sweet potatoes—Peeled and cut into 1-inch cubes
- Carrots—Peeled and cut into 1-inch chunks
- White turnips or rutabagas (yellow turnips)—Peeled and cut into 1-inch cubes
- Parsnips—Peeled and cut into 1-inch chunks
- Butternut or other winter squash—Peeled and cut into 1-inch cubes
- Cauliflower—Cut into large florets

Spice Blends (Pick 1)

- 2 tablespoons curry powder
- 2 tablespoons garam masala
- Cumin Spice Mix—2 teaspoons ground cumin, 2 teaspoons paprika, $\frac{1}{4}$ teaspoon cayenne pepper (or red pepper flakes)
- Warm Spice Mix—2 teaspoons ground ginger, $\frac{1}{2}$ teaspoon nutmeg, $\frac{1}{4}$ teaspoon cayenne pepper (or red pepper flakes)

pam's fave combos for creamy roasted vegetable soups

Carrots and curry powder

Cauliflower and Cumin Spice Mix

Parsnips and garam masala

Sweet potatoes or parsnips and Warm Spice Mix

notes and tips

- Cauliflower and root vegetables—perfect for roasting—work best here because they're substantial enough to thicken the soup on their own. Broccoli doesn't roast well, and most other vegetables require additional thickener.

- I frequently rely on evaporated milk for meatless cooking, and these soups are no exception. Evaporated milk offers the richness of cream without the calories.

- I rely on spice blends (as opposed to a single spice) to give the soups complexity. I suggest those that are readily available in the spice racks of most well-stocked grocery stores, but if you have favorite spice blends and favorite vegetables, chances are they're compatible.

- These soups are full flavored, but a little crunch garnish is often nice—sautéed pine nuts, roasted nuts, buttery toasted croutons. Apple chips are nice too.

- Preroasting the vegetables gives the soup depth; a brief simmer with aromatics melds the flavors. ➤

- Vent the blender cap to release pressure when pureeing the soup, covering the opening with a towel to avoid splatters. ➤

supper soup bars

For feeding a group with diverse appetites and tastes, a soup bar works nicely. You provide a flavorful broth and bowls of fixin's and everybody assembles his own bowl. There are two fun options here. The first is pho-meets-ramen noodle soup, the second, a build-your-own tortilla soup.

Start by making a quick vegetable broth—not from scratch. Simply simmer aromatics in a good quality vegetable broth (I offer suggestions in each recipe) for about 10 minutes. Just before serving, whisk in a little light miso for flavor. While the broth simmers, assemble your bar. Some things will need light cooking, but it's mostly just pulling ingredients from the pantry and fridge and spooning them into bowls. Then let everyone choose what they like from this colorful array of ingredients and condiments.

Although 3 quarts may seem like a lot of broth, I usually figure a scant 3 cups of broth per person. By the time it cooks down and everyone goes back for seconds, you may have a little leftover, but it won't be much. Since the ingredients going into the bowl are at room temperature, it's important that the broth be piping hot. Give everyone a big ladleful and then keep the pot covered and on low heat for those who might want seconds.

Don't use large shallow soup bowls, which cause the soup to cool too quickly. Small, deep bowls also encourage everyone to come back for a second round of flavorings and ingredients, so they can try a new combo.

Another bonus: There will likely be leftovers, which will help with meal prep later in the week.

master formula asian soup bar

3 quarts good-quality vegetable broth
(see Note)
6 thin coins (no need to peel) fresh
ginger, lightly smashed
1 bunch cilantro—16 stems,
plus ½ cup chopped leaves
1 bunch scallions—white parts left
whole, green parts thinly sliced
1 lime—3 long strips of zest removed,
lime cut into wedges
2 heaping cups Cooking Vegetables
(Pick 1 or more)
8 ounces Noodles (Pick 1)
7 to 8 ounces extra-firm tofu, patted dry
and cut into ½-inch cubes
1 heaping cup Raw Vegetables
(Pick 1 or more)
Soy sauce
6 tablespoons light (mellow white) miso

Combine the vegetable broth, ginger, cilantro stems, scallion whites, and lime zest in a large soup kettle. Bring to a simmer and then simmer for about 10 minutes longer to blend the flavors. Cover and keep warm.

Meanwhile, bring a generous 2 quarts of lightly salted water to a boil in a second pot. Add the Cooking Vegetable(s) and simmer until tender-crisp, about 3 minutes. With a slotted spoon, transfer the vegetables to a plate and set aside. Add the Noodles to the same pot and, using the suggested cooking times below as a guide, cook until tender. Drain and cool under running water to keep from sticking if not using right away.

Set out bowls of tofu, noodles, cooking vegetables, and Raw Vegetables, as well as a bottle of soy sauce and small bowls of scallion greens, chopped cilantro, and lime wedges.

When ready to serve, remove the solids from the broth with a slotted spoon, and discard. Whisk in the miso and return to a simmer. Be sure to get it piping hot.

After diners fill their bowls with tofu, noodles, vegetables, and condiments as desired, ladle in hot broth and serve with lime and soy passed separately.

Note: For this soup, a light-colored vegetable broth is needed, so my pick for a good-quality store-bought broth is Imagine vegetable broth. Although I like the taste of their No-Chicken style of vegetable broth, its hue is a little orange for this soup.

Serves 4 to 6

asian soup bar options

Cooking Vegetables (Pick 1 or more, totaling 2 heaping cups)

- Broccoli crowns—Stems thinly sliced, head cut into small florets
- Carrots—Peeled and thinly sliced
- Snow peas or sugar snap peas—Halved crosswise on the diagonal
- Thin asparagus—Cut into 1-inch lengths
- Thin green beans—Cut into 1-inch lengths

Noodles (Pick 1; 8 ounces pretty consistently cooks up to about 4 cups)

- Soba—Cooking time about 5 minutes
- Udon—Cooking time about 5 minutes
- Lo mein—Cooking time about 5 minutes
- Ramen noodles—(discard the flavoring packet) crushed into bite-size pieces: cooking time about 3 minutes.
- Thai rice stick noodles—Cover with boiling water, cover, and let stand until soft, about 5 minutes.
- Pasta (spaghetti, linguine, and even bite-size pasta shapes work fine here)—Cooking time varies; use package times as guides.

Raw Vegetables (Pick 1 or more)

- Radishes—Halved and thinly sliced
- Fresh bean sprouts
- Enoki mushrooms or stemmed and thinly sliced shiitake or white mushrooms
- Sliced canned water chestnuts—Drained and rinsed
- Bok choy—Very thinly sliced, white and green parts
- Napa cabbage—Halved, cored, and very thinly sliced

master formula tortilla soup bar

3 quarts good-quality vegetable broth
1 bunch cilantro—16 stems and ½ cup chopped leaves
1 bunch scallions—white parts left whole, green parts thinly sliced
6 sun-dried tomato halves
3 garlic cloves, halved
1 lime—3 long strips of zest removed, lime cut into wedges
1 jalapeño chile pepper, left whole
2 cups Base (Pick 1 or 2)
2 cups Cooked Vegetables (Pick 1)
1 cup Raw Vegetables (Pick 1 or 2)
Dairy Topping (Pick 1 or 2)
Heat (Pick 1 or 2)
1 bag (12 ounces) tortilla chips
6 tablespoons light (mellow white) miso

Combine the broth, cilantro stems, scallion whites, sun-dried tomatoes, garlic, lime zest, and jalapeño in a large soup kettle. Bring to a simmer and then simmer for about 10 minutes longer to blend the flavors. Cover and keep warm.

Meanwhile, warm the Base in the microwave or over low heat in a medium saucepan. Set out in a bowl and keep warm. Prepare the Cooked Vegetable and Raw Vegetables and set them out in bowls. Set out bowls of Dairy Topping, Heat, scallion greens, chopped cilantro, lime wedges, and tortilla chips.

When ready to serve, remove the solids from the broth with a slotted spoon, whisk in the miso, and return to a simmer. Be sure to get it piping hot.

After diners fill their bowls with the base and vegetables, ladle in the hot broth. Top as desired with tortilla chips, dairy, heat, scallions, cilantro, and lime.

Note: A base of corn, hominy, or beans makes this almost as substantial as chili. Since this soup has richer ingredients—cheese, tortilla chips, avocado—it will easily serve 6, especially if you increase the cheese to 6 ounces and add a few extra ingredients. So that it stays hot, serve the soup in small, deep bowls, keep the broth simmering, and encourage everyone to come back for seconds.

Serves 4 to 6 with leftovers

tortilla soup bar options

Base (Pick 1 or 2 for 2 cups total)

- Frozen corn, thawed
- Canned hominy, drained
- Canned or cooked pinto or black beans, drained

Cooked Vegetables (Pick 1)

- 2 small bell peppers—Your color choice, stemmed, cored, and thinly sliced and cooked in a generous tablespoon of oil with a sprinkling of salt, in a large skillet over medium-high heat until tender-crisp, about 5 minutes.
- 2 medium-small zucchini or yellow squash—Thinly sliced and cooked like the peppers.
- 2 heaping cups finely diced winter squash or sweet potato—Placed in a medium skillet along with $\frac{1}{3}$ cup water, 2 teaspoons oil, and a sprinkling of salt. Cook over high heat, covered, until just tender, 5 to 7 minutes.

Raw Vegetables (Pick 1 or 2 for 1 cup total)

- Cabbage—Any type, thinly sliced
- Radishes—Halved and thinly sliced
- Avocado—Cut into small dice
- Black ripe or pimiento-stuffed olives—Sliced or coarsely chopped (no more than $\frac{1}{2}$ cup)

Dairy Topping (Pick 1 or 2)

- Cheese—4 ounces grated pepper Jack or sharp Cheddar or crumbled queso fresco
- Reduced-fat sour cream—$\frac{1}{2}$ cup

Heat (Pick 1 or 2)

- Salsa—Regular and/or verde
- Hot pepper sauce—Red and/or green
- Fresh or pickled jalapeño, sliced
- Canned chopped green chiles

master formula minestrone for every season

2 quarts good-quality vegetable broth
1 can (14.5 ounces) petite-cut diced tomatoes
2 tablespoons olive oil
1 large onion, finely diced
1 large celery rib, finely diced
1 large carrot, finely diced
2 teaspoons Italian seasoning
$\frac{1}{4}$ to $\frac{1}{2}$ teaspoon red pepper flakes
2 cans (15 to 16 ounces each) small white beans, not drained
1 cup ditalini pasta
Seasonal Vegetables (Pick 1)
Salt and ground black pepper to taste
Grated Parmesan cheese (optional)

Stir broth and tomatoes together in a 2-quart glass measuring cup or other microwave-safe container and microwave on high power until steamy hot, about 5 minutes

Heat oil over medium-high heat in a large soup kettle. Add the onions, celery, and carrots and cook until tender, about 5 minutes. Add Italian seasoning and pepper flakes and cook until fragrant, about a minute longer. Add remaining ingredients except the Parmesan, cover, and bring to a simmer. Reduce heat to medium-low; continue to simmer, partially covered and stirring occasionally, until vegetables are soft and pasta is tender, about 15 minutes longer. Adjust the seasonings and serve hot topped with the cheese if using.

Serves 8

Seasonal Vegetables (Pick 1)

- **Fall: about 8 ounces each bite-size cauliflower florets and broccoli rabe, trimmed and chopped coarse**

- **Winter: about 8 ounces each shredded savoy cabbage and butternut squash, cut into medium dice**

- **Spring: about 8 ounces each frozen green peas and coarsely chopped escarole**

- **Summer: about 8 ounces each zucchini, cut into medium dice, and well-washed spinach, stemmed and coarsely chopped**

notes and tips

- Except for the true dog days of summer, I eat soup nearly year-round, so it's nice to have a formula that works for every season. And if you think soup isn't for supper, give this one a try. It's stick-to-your-ribs substantial.

- Don't limit yourself to the vegetables I've suggested. Some others to consider: green beans, leafy greens (both firm and tender), yellow squash, bell peppers. Just figure about 8 ounces each of 2 vegetables. Or create your own minestrone soup vegetable mix, using about 1 pound of vegetables in all.

classic soups made meatless

Converting some of my best-loved soups for meatless menus was a particularly satisfying exercise, but there are a few tricks beyond substituting vegetable stock for beef or chicken broth. When there's no meat in the pot, I find evaporated milk and, in some cases, heavy cream add richness and substance. Beer (preferably *not* of the nonalcoholic variety) adds depth, as with Creamy Beer Cheese Soup with Salsa Verde. Condiments can perk up any soup, but they play an especially important role in vegetarian ones. Salsa verde, for example, or hot red pepper sauce, Worcestershire, even ketchup, adds that extra dimension. Bold spices—cumin, paprika—help too, and if you can find smoked versions of either, even better.

Once you've nailed the flavorings, there are lots of hearty carbs and vegetables that give substance. Pasta couples with white beans to make stick-to-your-ribs protein in White Bean Noodle Soup. Lentils paired with potatoes (in Lentil Soup with Potatoes, Cumin, and Paprika) is a satisfying dinner. Mushrooms offer meaty mouth-feel in Mushroom Barley Soup.

With a few simple adjustments, most of the following soups could easily be converted back to the meaty original. After you've tasted a few of these, however, I doubt you'll go back.

mushroom barley soup

The combination of fresh and dried
mushrooms, along with the red miso
paste, give this soup bold flavor.

½ ounce dried mushrooms, chopped or
 broken into bite-size pieces
1 quart good-quality vegetable broth (see
 page 106)
2 tablespoons olive oil
1 large onion, cut into medium dice
1 pound sliced cremini mushrooms
¾ teaspoon dried thyme leaves
3 cups cooked barley (see page 268 for
 cooking instructions)
¼ cup red miso paste
Salt and ground black pepper

Stir the dried mushrooms and broth together in
a 2-quart glass measuring cup or other
microwave-safe container and microwave until
steamy hot and the mushrooms have softened,
about 5 minutes.

Meanwhile, heat the oil in a large soup kettle
over medium-high heat. Add the onion and
cook until golden brown, about 5 minutes. Add
the fresh mushrooms and cook until well
browned, 5 to 7 minutes. Add the thyme and
then the hot broth and barley and bring to a
simmer. Reduce the heat to medium-low and
simmer, partially covered and stirring
occasionally, for about 10 minutes to blend the
flavors.

Whisk in the miso, and if too thick, add water
to thin to desired thickness. Adjust the
seasonings, including salt and pepper to taste,
and serve hot.

Serves 4

just right corn chowder

Although I like the flavor of Kitchen Basics vegetable broth, its rich brown color is wrong for this soup. Stick with Imagine or Pacific brands here.

1 quart good-quality vegetable broth
1 generous tablespoon olive oil
1 large onion, cut into medium dice
$\frac{1}{2}$ red bell pepper, stemmed, cored, and cut into medium dice
$\frac{1}{4}$ cup all-purpose flour
3 medium boiling potatoes (about 1 pound), cut into medium dice
1 bag (16 ounces) frozen corn kernels
1 large bay leaf
$\frac{1}{2}$ teaspoon dried thyme leaves
$\frac{3}{4}$ cup heavy cream
2 tablespoons light (mellow white) miso
2 tablespoons chopped fresh parsley
Salt and ground black or white pepper

Combine the broth and 1 cup water in a 2-quart glass measuring cup or other microwave-safe container and microwave until the broth is hot, about 5 minutes.

Meanwhile, heat the oil in a soup kettle over medium-high heat. Add the onion and bell pepper and cook until soft, about 5 minutes.

Sprinkle with the flour and stir until lightly colored, 30 seconds to a minute. Add the hot broth, along with the potatoes, corn, bay leaf, and thyme. Simmer until the potatoes are tender, 10 to 15 minutes.

Whisk in the cream, miso, and parsley. Adjust the seasonings, including salt and pepper to taste, and return to a simmer. Serve hot.

Serves 6

creamy tomato soup with garam masala

Evaporated milk, not cream, makes this soup smooth and luxurious while saving calories. The addition of a small amount of baking soda helps neutralize the tomatoes' acid, which in turn prevents the milk from curdling. If you can't find garam masala, an Indian spice blend, substitute an equal amount of curry powder.

1 generous tablespoon vegetable oil
1 medium-large onion, chopped
1 tablespoon garam masala
1 can (28 ounces) crushed tomatoes
½ teaspoon baking soda
1 can (12 ounces) low-fat evaporated milk
Salt and ground black pepper

Heat the oil in a soup kettle over medium heat. Add the onion and cook until tender, about 5 minutes. Add the garam masala and cook until fragrant, about 30 seconds. Add the tomatoes and baking soda and bring to a simmer. Reduce the heat to low and simmer, partially covered, for about 5 minutes to blend the flavors.

Transfer the mixture to a blender and puree until creamy smooth, adding as much of the evaporated milk as will fit in the blender jar during processing. Return the soup to the pot, along with any remaining milk. Adjust seasonings, adding salt and pepper to taste. Bring to a simmer and serve hot.

Serves 4

chunky leek and potato soup

Here again, Kitchen Basics brand is a little dark and heavy for this light soup.

1 quart good-quality vegetable broth (e.g., Pacific or Imagine brand)
2 tablespoons unsalted butter
4 medium leeks, light green and white parts quartered lengthwise and cut into medium dice and thoroughly rinsed and drained (4 generous cups)
8 small red or Yukon Gold potatoes (about 1 pound), scrubbed and thinly sliced (about 4 cups)
½ cup heavy cream
¼ cup yellow miso

Combine the broth and 2 cups water in a 2-quart glass measuring cup or other microwave-safe container and microwave until the broth is hot, about 5 minutes.

Meanwhile, heat the butter in a soup kettle over medium heat. Add the leeks and cook until tender, 5 to 7 minutes. Add the potatoes and hot broth and bring to a simmer. Reduce the heat to medium-low and simmer, partially covered, until the potatoes are tender, 12 to 15 minutes.

Whisk in the cream, miso, and additional water, if necessary, to achieve desired consistency. Return to a simmer and serve hot.

Serves 4 to 6

black bean hominy chili

Don't feel locked into black beans here. I frequently make this soup with whatever beans I have around. I adore hominy, but if you can't find it or don't care for it, substitute frozen or fresh corn.

1 quart good-quality vegetable broth
1 can (14.5 ounces) petite-cut diced tomatoes
1 generous tablespoon vegetable oil
1 medium-large onion, cut into medium dice
1 bell pepper, any color, stemmed, cored, and cut into medium dice
3 tablespoons chili powder
1 teaspoon ground cumin
1 teaspoon dried oregano
2 cans (15.5 ounces each) black beans, drained
2 cans (15.5 ounces each) hominy, drained
3 large garlic cloves, minced
1 ounce bittersweet chocolate, chopped
1/4 cup chopped fresh cilantro

Stir together the broth and tomatoes in a 2-quart glass measuring cup or other microwave-safe container and microwave until steamy hot, about 5 minutes.

Meanwhile, heat the oil in a Dutch oven or small soup kettle over medium-high heat. Add the onion and pepper and cook until soft and golden brown, about 5 minutes. Add the chili powder, cumin, and oregano and cook until fragrant, a minute or so. Add the beans and hominy along with the hot broth mixture. Bring to a simmer, reduce the heat to low, and simmer, partially covered, until the vegetables are tender and the flavors have blended, about 20 minutes.

Stir in the garlic, chocolate, and cilantro and simmer a couple of minutes to blend the flavors. Remove from the heat and let stand a few minutes if there's time. Adjust the seasonings and serve hot.

Serves 4 to 6

◄ For bold flavor, stir the garlic, chocolate, and cilantro into the finished chili.

vegetable gumbo

In combination with the rice, pinto beans give the soup substance while red miso and Worcestershire boost flavor.

1 quart good-quality vegetable broth (see page 106)
1 can (14.5 ounces) petite-cut diced tomatoes
1 generous tablespoon vegetable oil
1 medium-large onion, cut into medium dice
2 medium celery ribs, cut into medium dice
½ green bell pepper, stemmed, cored, and cut into medium dice
1 tablespoon Cajun seasoning
½ teaspoon dried thyme leaves
8 to 10 ounces frozen cut okra*
2 cans (15.5 ounces each) pinto beans, not drained
¼ cup long-grain rice
1 tablespoon red miso
1 teaspoon vegetarian Worcestershire sauce
2 tablespoons chopped fresh parsley
Salt and ground black pepper

Combine the broth and tomatoes in a 2-quart glass measuring cup or other microwave-safe container and microwave until steamy hot, about 5 minutes.

Meanwhile, heat the oil in a Dutch oven or soup kettle over medium-high heat. Add the onion, celery, and bell pepper and cook until soft and golden brown, about 5 minutes. Add the Cajun seasoning and thyme and cook until fragrant, 30 seconds to a minute. Add the hot broth mixture, along with the okra, beans, and rice. Bring to a simmer, reduce the heat to medium-low, and simmer, partially covered, until the vegetables are tender and the flavors have blended, about 20 minutes.

Whisk in the miso, Worcestershire sauce, and parsley. Adjust the seasonings, including salt and black pepper to taste, and serve hot.

Serves 4 to 6

*Okra is usually sold in 1-pound bags or 10-ounce boxes, so use either a half bag or a full box here.

tortellini soup

Substitute an equal amount of spinach for the kale if you like.

1 quart good-quality vegetable broth (see page 106)
1 can (14.5 ounces) petite-cut diced tomatoes
1 generous tablespoon vegetable oil
1 medium-large onion, cut into medium dice
2 medium carrots, peeled and cut into medium dice
1 small zucchini, cut into medium dice
½ bell pepper, any color, stemmed, cored, and cut into medium dice
1 teaspoon Italian seasoning
8 lightly packed cups (about 8 ounces) stemmed and coarsely chopped kale
2 cups (about 9 ounces) bite-size cheese tortellini, fresh or frozen
Grated Parmesan cheese (preferably Reggiano), for passing

Combine the broth and tomatoes in a 2-quart glass measuring cup or other microwave-safe container and microwave until steamy hot, about 5 minutes.

Meanwhile, heat the oil in a Dutch oven or soup kettle over medium-high heat. Add the onion and carrots and cook until soft and golden brown, about 5 minutes. Stir in the zucchini, peppers, and Italian seasoning and cook until fragrant, a minute or so. Add the hot broth mixture and 1 cup of water and bring to a simmer. Reduce the heat to medium-low and simmer, partially covered, for about 10 minutes.

Add the kale, stirring until it wilts, and cook, partially covered, about 5 minutes longer. Stir in the tortellini and cook, partially covered, until the tortellini are tender and their starch has lightly thickened the soup, about 7 minutes longer. Serve hot with Parmesan cheese passed separately.

Serves 4 to 6

french onion soup

The combination of miso, vegetable broth, and caramelized onions creates such a flavorful soup that I doubt I'll ever make this soup with meat broth again. The dark, rich color and caramelized-onion flavor of Kitchen Basics makes it the perfect broth for this soup.

2 tablespoons butter
2 tablespoons olive oil, plus extra oil for brushing bread
4 large sweet onions (about 2½ pounds), halved and thinly sliced
1 quart good-quality vegetable broth (preferably Kitchen Basics)
2 tablespoons all-purpose flour
¼ cup sweet vermouth
¼ cup red miso
18 slices (½ inch thick) cut from a baguette
6 slices Swiss or provolone cheese (about 4 ounces)
6 tablespoons grated Parmesan cheese

Heat the butter and 2 tablespoons oil in a soup kettle over high heat. Add the onions and cook, stirring often, until dramatically reduced and a light caramel brown, about 10 minutes. Reduce the heat to medium and continue to cook onions, stirring frequently, until rich caramel, 10 to 15 minutes longer.

Meanwhile, microwave broth in a 2-quart glass measuring cup or other microwave-safe container until piping hot, about 5 minutes.

When the onions are fully cooked, sprinkle with the flour. Stir in the vermouth and then the hot broth. Bring to a boil, reduce to a simmer, and cook, partially covered, for about 5 minutes to blend the flavors. Whisk in the miso, adding water as necessary to achieve a lightly thickened soup.

When ready to serve, adjust the oven rack to the middle position and turn on the broiler. Lightly brush both sides of the bread slices with oil and arrange on a baking sheet. Toast under the broiler, turning once, until golden brown on both sides, a couple of minutes per side.

Place 6 ovenproof soup bowls (the diameter should be only slightly larger than the cheese slice or cut cheese to fit) on a sturdy rimmed baking sheet. Ladle the hot soup into the bowls. Top each with 3 toasts, a cheese slice, and then grated Parmesan. Broil until the cheese is melted and spotty brown, 2 to 3 minutes.

Serves 6

creamy beer cheese soup with salsa verde

This soup is rich—a small serving will fill you up. But if you'd like to bulk it up a bit, add steamed small broccoli florets to the finished soup, heat through, and serve. For a silky textured soup, you can puree it in the blender, but I like the texture the onions and salsa verde offer this otherwise creamy soup.

1 generous tablespoon canola oil
1 large onion, cut into medium dice
¼ cup all-purpose flour
2 cups good-quality vegetable broth (see page 106)
1 bottle or can (12 ounces) beer
½ cup salsa verde
1 large garlic clove, minced
1 teaspoon vegetarian Worcestershire sauce
8 ounces extra-sharp Cheddar cheese, grated (about 3 cups)
½ cup evaporated milk
Salt and ground black pepper

Heat the oil in a soup kettle over medium-high heat. Add the onion and cook until tender, about 5 minutes. Stir in the flour, and then the broth and beer, stirring constantly until the foaming subsides. Bring to a boil, reduce to a simmer, and cook, partially covered, for about 8 minutes to blend the flavors.

Stir in the salsa verde, garlic, and Worcestershire sauce and cook a couple of minutes longer. Whisk in the cheese until incorporated. Whisk in the evaporated milk and simmer to heat through. Adjust the seasonings, including salt and pepper to taste, and serve hot.

Serves 4

quick and hearty white bean noodle soup

Though not as rich as chicken pot pie, this soup will certainly remind you of it.

1 quart good-quality vegetable broth (see page 106)
1 can (12 ounces) evaporated milk
1 generous tablespoon vegetable oil
1 large onion, cut into medium dice
2 large carrots, peeled and cut into medium-small dice
2 large celery ribs, cut into medium-small dice
$\frac{1}{2}$ teaspoon dried thyme leaves
2 cans (15.5 ounces each) white beans, not drained
2 generous cups wide egg noodles
1 cup (5 ounces) frozen green peas
$\frac{1}{4}$ cup chopped fresh parsley (optional)
Salt and ground black pepper

Combine the broth and evaporated milk in a 2-quart glass measuring cup or other microwave-safe container and microwave until steamy hot, about 5 minutes.

Heat the oil in a large soup kettle over medium-high heat. Add the onion, carrots, and celery and cook until softened, 5 to 7 minutes. Add the thyme, hot broth mixture, and beans and bring to a boil. Reduce the heat to a simmer and cook, partially covered, for about 15 minutes to blend the flavors.

Add the noodles, partially cover, and continue to simmer until tender, 8 to 10 minutes, stirring in the peas and parsley for the last few minutes of cooking. Adjust the seasonings, including a generous sprinkling of salt and pepper, and serve hot.

Serves 4 to 6

vegetable soup, brunswick-style

Most of the same ingredients—corn, lima beans, potatoes, and a little ketchup—are in this classic Southern soup, just no meat! And it's great.

1 quart good-quality vegetable broth (see page 106)
1 can (14.5 ounces) petite-cut diced tomatoes
⅓ cup ketchup
1 generous tablespoon vegetable oil
1 medium-large onion, chopped
2 medium celery ribs, cut into medium-small dice
2 carrots, peeled and cut into rounds or half rounds
1 teaspoon dried basil
½ teaspoon dried thyme leaves
8 ounces frozen corn
8 ounces frozen lima beans
1 pound (about 3 medium) red potatoes, cut into medium dice
½ cup evaporated milk
Salt and ground black pepper

Combine the broth, tomatoes, and ketchup in a 2-quart glass measuring cup or other microwave-safe container and microwave until steamy hot, about 5 minutes.

Meanwhile, heat the oil in a Dutch oven or small soup kettle over medium-high heat. Add the onion, celery, and carrots and cook until softened, about 5 minutes. Add the basil, thyme, hot broth mixture, corn, lima beans, and potatoes. Bring to a simmer, reduce the heat to low, and simmer, partially covered, until the vegetables are tender and the flavors have blended, about 20 minutes.

Stir in the evaporated milk. Adjust the seasonings, including salt and pepper to taste, and serve hot.

Serves 4 to 6

lentil soup with potatoes, cumin, and paprika

By cooking the lentils while the soup vegetables cook, you shave a good half hour off the cooking time.

1 pound (a generous 2 cups) lentils, rinsed
1 quart good-quality vegetable broth (see page 106)
2 tablespoons olive oil
1 large onion, cut into medium-large dice
2 medium carrots, peeled and cut into medium-large dice
2 medium celery ribs, cut into medium-large dice
1 tablespoon unsalted butter
2 medium garlic cloves, sliced
Pinch of sugar
2 teaspoons ground cumin (smoked, if you can find it)
2 teaspoons paprika (smoked, if you can find it)
4 small red potatoes, cut into medium dice
$\frac{1}{4}$ cup red miso
Salt and ground black pepper

Combine the lentils, broth, and 1 quart of water in a large saucepan. Bring to a boil, reduce to a simmer, and cook, partially covered, until the lentils are tender but still with a little chew, about 20 minutes.

Meanwhile, heat the oil in a large skillet over medium-high heat. Add the onion, carrots, and celery and cook, stirring frequently, until most of their liquid evaporates and the vegetables start to brown, about 6 minutes. Reduce the heat to medium-low and add the butter, garlic, and sugar. Spread the vegetables in a single layer and continue to cook, stirring occasionally, until they turn a rich brown color, about 10 minutes. Stir in the cumin and paprika and cook until fragrant, about 30 seconds.

Add the lentils (and their cooking liquid) and the potatoes. Bring to a simmer and cook, partially covered, until the potatoes and lentils are tender and the soup has thickened, 10 to 15 minutes.

Whisk in the miso, then add water as needed to achieve desired consistency. Adjust the seasonings, including salt and pepper to taste, and serve hot.

Serves 6

variation: split pea soup with potatoes and caraway

Substitute an equal amount of split peas for the lentils and $1\frac{1}{2}$ teaspoons caraway seeds toasted in a small dry skillet until fragrant and then ground (a rolling pin works well) for the cumin and paprika.

skillet stews

We all need a dish we can throw together on the spur of the moment, no matter how barren the pantry and fridge. That's when skillet stews—soupier than a chili, more substantial than a chowder—are just the thing. Oil—check. Onion, celery, carrot—that's easy. Herbs and/or spices—got 'em all. Beans and grains—yes and yes. Petite-cut diced tomatoes and vegetable broth—my new pantry staples. Parsley or cilantro—almost always.

Here's how it goes. Sauté onions, celery, and carrots in a large skillet. Depending on the dish you've chosen, add the suggested herbs and/or spices. For Cajun Pinto Beans and Rice, it's Cajun seasonings and a little dried thyme. For Lentil and Potato Stew or Pasta e Fagioli, stir in common herb blends like Italian seasoning or herbes de Provence. If it's Indian, you've got your choice of curry or garam masala. Black Bean and Hominy Stew gets a kick from chili powder.

Once the spices are fragrant, add vegetable broth, tomatoes, and your choice of grains/legumes/starchy vegetables. Simmer for 15 to 20 minutes, stir in the parsley or cilantro, set the skillet on the table, and let everyone dig in. It's hard to believe an extraordinary dish could come from such ordinary ingredients.

master formula skillet stew

1 tablespoon olive oil
1 medium onion, cut into medium dice
1 celery rib, cut into medium dice
1 carrot, cut into medium dice
Herb/Spice Blends (Pick 1)
Grains/Legumes/Starchy Vegetables
   (Pick 2)
1 can (14.5 ounces) petite-cut
   diced tomatoes
2 cups to 1 quart vegetable broth,
   depending on your chosen grain
¼ cup parsley or cilantro
Salt and ground black pepper

Heat the oil in a 12-inch skillet over medium-high heat. Add the onion, celery, and carrot and cook until the onion is tender, about 5 minutes. Stir in the Herb/Spice Blend, followed by the Grains/Legumes/Starchy Vegetables, and finally the tomatoes and broth. Stirring occasionally, bring to a simmer. Reduce the heat to medium-low, cover, and simmer, stirring occasionally, until the ingredients are tender and the flavors have blended, 15 to 20 minutes.

Stir in the parsley or cilantro, adjust the seasonings, including salt and pepper to taste, and serve hot.

Serves 6

skillet stew options

Herb/Spice Blends (Pick 1)

- 2 tablespoons curry powder
- 2 tablespoons garam masala
- 2 tablespoons chili powder
- 1 tablespoon Italian seasoning
- 1 tablespoon herbes de Provence
- 4 teaspoons Cajun seasoning and ½ teaspoon dried thyme leaves
- Cumin Spice Mix: 4 teaspoons ground cumin, 2 teaspoons ground coriander, and 2 teaspoons dried oregano

Grain/Legumes/Starchy Vegetables (Pick 2)

The grains, legumes, and starches you choose will determine how much broth you use (2 cups or 1 quart). Pasta, rice, lentils, and quinoa all need liquid to cook and soften, so for these use the full quart of broth. The last items on the list—canned beans, hominy, corn, peas, and potatoes—absorb little moisture and need only 2 cups. If using a combination of these types—rice and peas, for example—use the full quart.

- 2 cups small pasta, such as ditalini
- 1 cup white or basmati rice
- 1 cup lentils
- 1 cup quinoa
- 2 cans (15 to 16 ounces each) beans—small white beans, chickpeas, pinto beans, hominy, or black beans—drained (black beans need a rinse as well)
- 2 cans (15 to 16 ounces each) hominy, drained
- 2 cups fresh or frozen corn
- 2 cups fresh or frozen peas
- 1 pound red potatoes, sweet potatoes, or yams—peeled and cut into medium dice

pam's fav combos for meatless skillet stews

Cajun Pinto Beans and Rice: 4 teaspoons Cajun seasoning and ½ teaspoon dried thyme leaves, pinto beans and white rice (use 1 quart broth), parsley. Set out bottles of hot sauce for those who want extra spice.

Lentil and Potato Stew: herbes de Provence, lentils and red potatoes (use 1 quart broth), parsley.

Pasta e Fagioli: Italian seasoning, small white beans and ditalini (use 1 quart broth), parsley. For extra flavor, grate a little Parmesan cheese over each bowl.

Black Bean and Hominy Stew: chili powder, black beans and hominy, cilantro. Serve this stew with your favorite salsa, freshened up, if you like, with a little chopped fresh cilantro and a squirt of lime juice.

Chickpeas and Yam Stew with Garam Masala: garam masala, chickpeas and yams (or sweet potatoes), cilantro. This stew deviates slightly from the template by replacing half the vegetable broth with coconut milk.

Peruvian Quinoa and Corn Stew: Cumin Spice Mix, quinoa and corn (use 1 quart broth), cilantro.

Curried Quinoa (or Lentils) and Peas: curry powder, quinoa and peas (use 1 quart broth), cilantro.

notes and tips

- If you want to speed up the cooking process, microwave the petite-cut diced tomatoes and broth in a 2-quart glass measuring cup or other microwave-safe container while the vegetables cook.

- Replacing half the vegetable broth with coconut milk adds great flavor to any Indian-style skillet stew. ➤

super sandwiches

For all you vegetarians who've come to rely on frozen veggie burgers, hummus, and pita breads, this chapter will delightfully broaden your options. There's a burger formula, so if, in fact, you want to eat a different burger every night of the week you can, and the sandwiches are fun any time of the day. So try giving up deli meats for a month and give these sandwiches a go. You might find yourself eating in a completely different way . . . and loving it.

really simple bean burgers

If you think a thick juicy beef burger is the one dish you could never give up, try these bean burgers. Over the years I've made many grain, bean, and veggie burgers that just weren't worth the effort. Not these. You'll find really simple, really delicious burgers come together almost as quickly as it takes to flavor and form beef patties.

Best of all, the only simpler vegetarian burgers you'll find are the ones in the freezer case. No need to cook grains, beans, or vegetables—it's just 2 cans of drained beans—1 mashed, 1 left whole—bound with dried breadcrumbs and eggs. The mix of whole beans and mashed works well, the whole beans providing texture, the mashed ones binding the patties.

As with regular burgers, you've got a choice of cooking method—stovetop or grill—and the flavoring and topping possibilities for these bean burgers are endless.

master formula
really simple bean burgers

2 cans (15.5 ounces each) black, white, or pinto beans or black-eyed peas
1 cup dried breadcrumbs
2 large eggs, lightly beaten
1 teaspoon coarsely ground black pepper
½ teaspoon garlic powder
Extra Flavorings (see Burger options)
6 good-quality hamburger buns

Drain 1 can of beans, reserving the liquid, and mash the beans in a medium bowl. Drain the second can, add to the bowl with the breadcrumbs, eggs, pepper, and garlic powder. Stir in Extra Flavorings if using. If necessary, add a little of the bean liquid until the mixture holds together but is not wet. Divide into 6 equal portions and shape into 4-inch patties.

Warm the buns in a 300°F oven for about 5 minutes. Meanwhile, heat ¼ cup olive or canola oil in a large (12-inch) skillet over medium-high heat. Add the patties and cook, turning only once, until a crisp brown crust forms on both sides, about 6 minutes total. If you've chosen a burger that gets topped with cheese, add it now. Cover the skillet, turn the heat to low, and let the burgers continue to cook until the cheese melts. Top the burgers as desired.

(If you prefer to cook the burgers on the grill, see Grill Method, page 150.)

Makes 6 burgers

burger options

(use these extra flavorings to embellish the basic burger)

- **The Classic:** Make the burgers without any extra flavoring and cook according to Stovetop or Grill Method, topping the burgers with 6 thin slices of sharp Cheddar cheese when instructed. Stir together $\frac{1}{2}$ cup mayonnaise and 1 tablespoon coarse-grain mustard; spread over warm buns and dress the burgers with green leaf lettuce, lightly salted tomato slices, and thinly sliced red onion. Serve with ketchup.

- **The Southwestern:** Mix in $\frac{1}{2}$ cup prepared salsa, 1 teaspoon ground cumin, and $\frac{1}{4}$ cup chopped fresh cilantro before forming the burgers. Cook burgers according to Stovetop or Grill Method. Mix 2 mashed avocados with $\frac{1}{2}$ cup mayonnaise, 2 teaspoons fresh lime juice, and salt and pepper to taste. Spread over warm buns and dress the burgers with lightly salted sliced tomatoes and thinly sliced red onion.

- **The Neapolitan:** Mix in $\frac{1}{4}$ cup chopped fresh basil leaves and 1 tablespoon balsamic vinegar before forming the burgers. Cook the burgers according to the Stovetop or Grill Method, topping the burgers with 6 slices mozzarella cheese when instructed. Stir together a generous $\frac{1}{4}$ cup mayonnaise and $\frac{1}{4}$ cup pesto. Spread over warm buns and dress the burgers with lightly salted sliced tomatoes.

- **The Curry:** Mix in $\frac{1}{4}$ cup chopped fresh cilantro, $\frac{1}{4}$ cup Major Grey's chutney (mincing any large mango pieces), and 1 tablespoon curry powder before forming the burgers. Cook the burgers according to the Stovetop or Grill Method. Spread chutney over warm buns. Dress the burgers with cilantro and pickled carrots (4 peeled and coarsely grated medium carrots tossed with 4 teaspoons rice vinegar and a big pinch of salt).

- **The Cajun:** Mix in 1 tablespoon fresh thyme leaves, 2 tablespoons vegetarian Worcestershire sauce, and 2 teaspoons Cajun spice before forming the burgers. Cook the burgers according to the Stovetop or Grill Method. Dress the burgers with slaw (4 cups shredded cabbage mixed with $\frac{1}{2}$ cup finely diced bell pepper, 2 thinly sliced scallions, 3 tablespoons mayonnaise, 4 teaspoons cider vinegar, and 2 teaspoons Cajun seasoning).

- **The Tahini:** Mix in $\frac{1}{4}$ cup fresh cilantro, 2 tablespoons tahini, 1 teaspoon ground coriander, and 1 teaspoon ground cumin before forming the burgers. Cook the burgers according to the Stovetop or Grill Method. Dress the burgers with tzatziki (1 hothouse cucumber—grated and squeezed dry—mixed with 1 cup 2% Greek yogurt, 2 minced garlic cloves, 4 teaspoons red wine vinegar, and salt and pepper to taste).

- **The Five-Spice:** Mix in $\frac{1}{4}$ cup fresh cilantro, 3 tablespoons soy sauce, 2 teaspoons sugar, 2 teaspoons rice vinegar, 1 teaspoon toasted sesame oil, and $1\frac{1}{2}$ teaspoons five-spice powder before forming the burgers. Cook the burgers according to the Stovetop or Grill Method. Spread the buns with Thai sweet chili sauce. Dress the burgers with cilantro sprigs and pickled cucumber (1 thinly sliced hothouse cucumber, 2 tablespoons rice vinegar, 2 teaspoons sugar, and salt to taste).

variation: grill method

Heat all burners of a gas grill on high. Lightly brush the tops of the patties with oil. Place the patties on the hot rack, oiled side down, cover, and grill until spotty brown, about 3 minutes. Lightly brush the tops with oil and flip the burgers. Replace the cover and continue to grill until the burgers are spotty brown on the second side, about 3 minutes longer. If you've chosen a burger that gets topped with cheese, add it now. Place the buns on the grill rack, turn off the heat, and let burgers and buns continue to cook until the cheese melts and the buns are warm. Top the burgers as desired.

notes and tips

• Not every type of bean works for these. When you are using a mix of mashed and whole, the smaller ones, like black beans, white beans, pinto beans, and black-eyed peas, hold together better than bigger legumes like cannellini beans and chickpeas.

• You can add fresh herbs, spices, and flavorings as seen in many of the variations, but the classic is flavored simply—just garlic powder and black pepper—and since most canned beans have already been seasoned, there's no need to add salt.

• For an even quicker bean burger, substitute 1 can (16 ounces) vegetarian refried beans for one of the cans of beans and reduce the eggs from 2 to 1.

• Fork mashing 1 can of the beans helps the patties keep their shape; leaving the second can whole lends appealing texture to the burgers. ➤

classic sandwiches made meatless

Many recipes can be reduced to a simple technique or formula. The sandwiches in this section can't be. They're here because they're phenomenal versions of a meaty favorite. Most of them are so substantial and rib-sticking that a half will satisfy smaller appetites; a whole sub should make even the hungriest diner very happy.

If given the choice between regular meatballs and the toasted garlic- and feta-flavored ones in Spinach Meatball Subs, I'd definitely go for the latter. And in Eggplant Parmesan Sandwiches, crisp meaty eggplant rivals chicken cutlets in flavor and reigns in value.

Mushrooms stand in for beef in two delicious favorites—Mushroom Sandwiches au Jus and Philly Cheese Steak-less Sandwiches.

In Meatless BLTs an unlikely duo of smoked mozzarella and crumbled pita chips mimic bacon, and lentils are almost a dead ringer for ground meat in Meatless Sloppy Joes. With all the familiar Reuben fixin's—sauerkraut, Swiss cheese, and Russian dressing— you'll never guess a hash brown patty replaces the corned beef in my version.

The same is true for Meatless Cubans. Teamed with ballpark mustard, dill pickles, and Swiss cheese, a cumin-flavored kidney bean patty makes a convincing substitute for pork. In Meatless Muffulettas salty, meaty artichoke hearts and sun-dried tomatoes are credible stand-ins for cold cuts when surrounded by the olive salad and two cheeses in the classic sandwich.

And finally, stuff a warm pita bread with potatoes that have been crushed with roasted garlic and some pungent feta topped with tzatziki and all the fixin's, and you've got a gyro that will surprise even serious carnivores.

spinach meatball subs

Doubling the spinach meatballs and tomato sauce will set you up with a meal for later in the week. Just warm up the meatballs in a pot of the sauce and serve over pasta.

Olive oil, for greasing the pan
2 large garlic cloves
2 packages (10 ounces each) frozen chopped
  spinach, thawed and squeezed dry
2 tablespoons butter, melted
½ cup crumbled feta cheese (a generous
  2 ounces)
¼ cup grated Parmesan cheese
¾ cup dried breadcrumbs
½ teaspoon dried oregano
Salt and ground black pepper
2 large eggs
4 Portuguese or submarine sandwich rolls
  (6 inches long), split almost all the way
  through
2 cups Simplest Tomato Sauce (recipe follows)
  or your favorite marinara sauce
8 thin slices mozzarella cheese (6 ounces)
½ cup crumbled feta or grated Parmesan
  (optional)

Adjust an oven rack to the lower-middle position and preheat the oven to 350°F. Coat a large rimmed baking sheet with olive oil.

Heat a small skillet over medium-high heat. Add the garlic and toast until spotty brown, about 5 minutes. Transfer the garlic to a cutting board, smash, and mince.

Break the spinach up into a medium bowl. With a fork, mix in the butter, cheeses, breadcrumbs, oregano, a scant ½ teaspoon salt, and several grinds of pepper. Beat the eggs and garlic; mix into the spinach mixture with a fork until thoroughly combined. Form the spinach mixture into about twenty-four 2-tablespoon balls and arrange on the baking sheet. Roast until firm, about 20 minutes. Remove from the oven. Turn the oven to broil (leaving the oven rack in the lower-middle position).

Open the rolls and place them on the baking sheet. Arrange 3 spinach balls on each roll half. Top with the tomato sauce and 2 slices of mozzarella per sandwich. Broil until the exposed bread is golden brown and the cheese is melted, 2 to 3 minutes. Sprinkle with additional feta or Parmesan if you like. Close up the rolls, cut the sandwiches in half, and serve.

Makes 4 large sandwiches, serving 4 to 8

the simplest
tomato sauce

There are endless ways to riff on this tomato sauce. If you've got over-the-hill red wine, use it to thin the sauce instead of water. For a little heat, add $\frac{1}{4}$ teaspoon red pepper flakes along with the oil and garlic. For a little more flavor, add a big pinch of dried basil, oregano, or Italian seasoning.

2 tablespoons pure olive oil
3 garlic cloves, minced
1 can (28 ounces) crushed or ground peeled
  tomatoes

Heat the oil and garlic in a large saucepan or Dutch oven over medium-high heat. Cook until the garlic starts to sizzle and turn golden. Add the tomatoes and their liquid and enough water to make a thin sauce (the amount of water you need will depend on the brand of tomatoes). Simmer to blend flavors and reduce to pasta sauce consistency, about 10 minutes.

Makes about 3 cups

eggplant parmesan sandwiches

Setting the fried eggplant slices on a rack set over a rimmed baking sheet keeps them from becoming soggy. If you'd like to make eggplant Parmesan sans bread, leave the eggplant on the rack and top with the mozzarella and Parmesan. Set the pan on the lower-middle oven rack and broil until the cheese melts and is spotty brown. Serve with spaghetti tossed with Simplest Tomato Sauce (page 155), saving a little of the sauce to spoon over the eggplant.

4 tablespoons olive oil
2 large eggs, beaten
½ teaspoon salt and ground black pepper
¾ cup dried breadcrumbs or panko
1 medium-large eggplant, sliced crosswise into ½-inch-thick rounds
4 Portuguese or submarine sandwich rolls (6 inches long), split almost all the way through
2 cups Simplest Tomato Sauce (page 155) or your favorite marinara sauce
8 thin slices mozzarella (6 ounces)
½ cup grated Parmesan cheese

Heat 2 tablespoons of the oil in a 12-inch skillet over low heat. Beat the eggs, salt, and a few grinds of pepper in a shallow dish. Spread the breadcrumbs in a separate shallow dish. Dip the eggplant slices first in the egg and then in the breadcrumbs, setting them on a rack set over newspaper.

A couple of minutes from frying, increase the heat to medium-high. When wisps of smoke start to rise from the pan, add as many eggplant slices as will fit in a single layer; fry, turning them only once, until rich golden brown, about 6 minutes total. Return the fried slices to the rack. Heat the remaining 2 tablespoons oil and coat and fry the remaining eggplant.

Meanwhile, adjust an oven rack to the lower-middle position and preheat the broiler. Open the rolls and place them on a rimmed baking sheet. Top each roll bottom with a portion of eggplant, tomato sauce, mozzarella, and Parmesan; broil until the cheese melts, 2 to 3 minutes. Close up the sandwiches, halve, and serve.

Makes 4 large sandwiches serving 4 to 8

mushroom sandwiches au jus

Meaty mushrooms make a substantial stand-in for roast beef in this meatless twist on a French dip.

2 tablespoons olive oil
1½ pounds sliced mushrooms
Salt and ground black pepper
4 large garlic cloves, minced
1½ teaspoons minced fresh rosemary
1½ tablespoons all-purpose flour
½ cup dry vermouth
⅔ cup evaporated milk
4 Portuguese rolls or other long soft buns
  (6 inches), split almost all the way through
4 thin slices Swiss cheese (3 ounces)

Adjust an oven rack to the middle position and preheat the broiler to high.

Heat the oil in a large skillet over medium-high heat. Add the mushrooms and cook without stirring for the first 2 to 3 minutes, allowing the mushrooms on the bottom to brown. Season to taste with salt and pepper and cook until golden brown, about 5 minutes longer, stirring occasionally. Add the garlic and rosemary and cook until fragrant. Sprinkle evenly with the flour. Whisk in the vermouth and then the milk. Bring to a simmer and cook to a thick sauce consistency, 1 to 2 minutes.

Meanwhile, place the buns on a baking sheet and toast until golden brown and crisp. Spoon a portion of mushrooms onto each bun bottom and top with cheese. Broil until the cheese melts, 1 to 2 minutes. Cap with the bun tops, halve, and serve.

Serves 4

meatless sloppy joes

Lentils are a wonderfully tasty and healthy substitute for ground meat. Because the mixture refrigerates and freezes well, go ahead and make the full pound. Leftovers can also be tossed with greens for an impromptu main course salad.

1 pound brown lentils
2 tablespoons vegetable oil
1 medium-large onion, chopped
1 cup ketchup
¼ cup Dijon mustard
2 tablespoons soy sauce
1 tablespoon vegetarian Worcestershire sauce
1 teaspoon hot red pepper sauce
2 tablespoons brown sugar
1 teaspoon garlic powder
Large sandwich buns

Bring 5 cups of water and the lentils to a boil in a covered 12-inch skillet. Reduce the heat to medium and cook until the water is almost absorbed and the lentils are just tender, 12 to 15 minutes.

Meanwhile, heat the oil in a second skillet over medium-high heat. Add the onions and cook until tender, about 5 minutes.

When the lentils are just tender, add the cooked onion, ketchup, mustard, soy sauce, Worcestershire, hot pepper sauce, brown sugar, and garlic powder and mix well. Cook, stirring frequently, for 5 minutes to blend the flavors. Mound the lentil mixture onto buns and serve.

Enough for up to 12 sandwiches

meatless blts

The combination of smoked mozzarella and crumbled pita chips beautifully mimic bacon's smoky crunch. If you can't find smoked mozzarella, try another smoky cheese.

¼ small red onion, grated
½ cup mayonnaise, regular or light
1 tablespoon Dijon mustard, preferably whole-grain
8 slices good-quality white sandwich bread, toasted
8 romaine lettuce leaves, torn into large pieces
2 large tomatoes, thinly sliced and lightly salted
8 ounces smoked mozzarella, thinly sliced
½ cup crumbled plain pita chips

Mix the onion, mayonnaise, and mustard in a small bowl.

Spread a portion of the mayonnaise mixture on each piece of toast and top with lettuce. Top 4 of the toast slices with tomatoes, cheese, and pita chips; cap with the remaining 4 toast slices. Halve and serve.

Serves 4

potato reubens

When I'm feeling especially ambitious, I make these with a filling of homemade rösti potatoes. The rest of the time I opt for store-bought hash brown patties, and the sandwich is still delicious. Use any hash brown patties left in the box to make Chopped Egg Caesar with Hash Brown Croutons (page 99).

½ cup mayonnaise, regular or light
2 tablespoons prepared cocktail sauce
¼ medium red onion, grated
3 tablespoons olive oil
6 store-bought hash brown patties
4 Portuguese or submarine sandwich rolls
   (6 inches long), split
6 thin slices Swiss cheese (4½ ounces)
1 pound sauerkraut, drained

Mix the mayonnaise, cocktail sauce, and onion in a small bowl. Set aside.

Heat the oil in a large skillet over medium heat. Add the hash brown patties and cook, partially covered and turning once, until hot, crisp, and golden brown, about 10 minutes. Reduce the heat to low while you assemble the sandwiches.

Spread the cut sides of each roll with the sauce. Arrange 1½ cheese slices on each roll bottom, followed by a portion of sauerkraut and then 1½ hash brown patties. Cap with the roll tops.

Increase the heat under the skillet to medium and arrange the sandwiches in the skillet, topping them with a plate. Place a 2-pound weight (a 1-quart carton of broth works well) on top of the plate. Cook, turning once, until the cheese melts and the sandwiches are crisp, 8 to 10 minutes total. Halve and serve.

Makes 4 large sandwiches, serving 4 to 8

meatless cubans

Pair the traditional mustard, dill pickle, and cheese of a classic Cubano sandwich with a quick, flavorful bean patty and you'll be pleasantly surprised at how much the meatless version tastes like the original. You can cook up to 4 sandwiches at a time in the skillet, but if you want to make all 6 at once, you'll need to fire up a second medium skillet or switch to a large griddle or heavy-duty roasting pan set over two burners. And there's always the option of cooking in batches or using a panini press.

3 tablespoons pure olive oil
1 can (16 ounces) vegetarian refried beans
1 can (15 to 16 ounces) light kidney beans, drained
1 cup dried breadcrumbs
1 teaspoon ground cumin
½ teaspoon garlic powder
1 large egg
4 Portuguese or submarine sandwich rolls (6 inches long), split
¼ cup ballpark mustard
12 thin slices Swiss cheese (9 ounces)
24 dill pickle sandwich slices

Heat the oil in large skillet over low heat while you make the patties. Mix the refried and whole beans in a bowl. Stir in the breadcrumbs, cumin, and garlic powder. Mix in the egg. Form the mixture into 6 oval patties about 5 by 3 inches.

Increase the heat under the skillet to medium-high and heat another minute or two. When wisps of smoke start to rise from the pan, add the patties and cook, turning only once, until crisp and golden brown, about 6 minutes total.

While the patties cook, spread the rolls with mustard. Arrange 1½ cheese slices and 2 pickle slices on each roll bottom and top.

Transfer the patties to a plate, leaving the skillet over low heat. Place a patty on each roll bottom; cap with roll tops. Increase the heat under the skillet to medium and add the sandwiches. Cover them with a plate topped with a 2-pound weight (a 1-quart carton of broth works well). Cook, turning once, until the cheese melts and sandwiches are crisp, 8 to 10 minutes total. Halve and serve.

Makes 6 large sandwiches

philly cheese steak-less sandwich

Worcestershire sauce adds an extra savory note to the mushrooms. You can use other varieties, but the portobello mushrooms best resemble the shaved beef in this all-American favorite.

4 Portuguese or hoagie rolls (6 inches long), split almost but not all the way through
3 tablespoons olive oil
1 large sweet onion, halved and thinly sliced
Salt and ground black pepper
½ cup jarred sweet fried peppers
1 pound portobello mushrooms, thinly sliced
1 tablespoon vegetarian Worcestershire sauce
4 slices provolone cheese (4 ounces)

Adjust an oven rack to the lower-middle position and preheat the oven to 300°F. Heat the buns until warm and soft.

Meanwhile, heat 1 tablespoon of the oil in a large skillet over medium-high heat. Add the onion, season with salt and black pepper, and cook until soft and golden, about 5 minutes. Add the fried peppers and continue cooking until the onions are a caramel brown, 2 to 3 minutes longer. Transfer to a plate.

Heat the remaining 2 tablespoons of oil in the same skillet. Add the mushrooms and cook without stirring for the first couple of minutes. Season with salt and pepper and cook, stirring, until golden brown, 3 to 4 minutes longer. Add the Worcestershire and cook for a minute or so to blend the flavors. Turn the heat to low, divide the mushrooms into 4 mounds, and top each mound with a slice of cheese. Cover the pan and heat until the cheese melts, 1 to 2 minutes.

Use a spatula to transfer one mound of mushrooms and cheese to each roll bottom and then top them with peppers and onions. Cap with a bun top, halve, and serve.

Serves 4

meatless muffulettas

The olive spread makes more than you'll need for 4 sandwiches, which is a good thing, because these sandwiches are so good you're gonna want to make them again soon. With extra olive spread in the fridge, the next time you crave one, it'll be as easy as making a ham sandwich. Fortunately the spread also keeps very well. Because I like the color and flavor contrast, I use mild black and piquant pimiento-stuffed green olives.

Olive Spread
2 medium garlic cloves
¼ cup drained capers
1 cup drained canned black olives
1 cup drained pimiento-stuffed salad olives
2 tablespoons red wine vinegar
2 teaspoons dried oregano
½ cup extra-virgin olive oil
½ cup finely chopped celery hearts

Sandwiches
4 Portuguese rolls or hoagie rolls (6 inches long), split and some of the crumb pulled from them to make a well
4 very thin slices mozzarella cheese
4 very thin slices provolone cheese
4 very thin slices pepper Jack cheese
½ red onion, thinly sliced
1 can (14 ounces) quartered artichoke hearts, drained and halved
¾ cup drained oil-packed sun-dried tomatoes, halved

To make the olive spread: Mince the garlic cloves in a food processor. Add the capers and pulse to chop. Add the olives, vinegar, and oregano; pulse to chop again. Transfer to a medium bowl and stir in the oil and celery. (The spread can be refrigerated in an airtight container for several weeks.)

To make the sandwiches: Spread 2 tablespoons of the olive spread on each half of each roll. Divide the cheese evenly among the sandwiches. On the bottom half of each sandwich, arrange a portion of onion, artichoke hearts, and sun-dried tomatoes. Cap with a roll top. Cut in half and serve.

Makes 4 large sandwiches, serving 4 to 8

Tips: If you don't want to invest in three cheeses, buy two varieties—pepper Jack and provolone, for example—and use 4 thick slices of each. You can also use marinated artichoke hearts here.

potato-feta gyros

"Sandwiching" the potato-garlic-cheese mixture between the lettuce and tomato means the ingredients are more evenly distributed, which results in a more pleasant eating experience.

1 cup plain 2% Greek yogurt
1 medium hothouse (seedless) cucumber, grated and squeezed dry
9 garlic cloves—8 whole, 1 minced
2 teaspoons plus 2 tablespoons olive oil
2 teaspoons fresh lemon juice
Salt and ground black pepper
¾ pound small red potatoes
1 cup crumbled feta cheese (4 ounces)
¼ medium red onion, finely diced
4 pita breads, preferably pocketless (8- or 9-inch)
2 cups shredded romaine lettuce hearts
1 cup finely diced tomatoes, lightly salted

Adjust an oven rack to the lower-middle position and preheat the oven to 350°F.

Combine the yogurt, cucumber, minced garlic, 2 teaspoons of the oil, the lemon juice, and a generous sprinkling of salt and pepper in a medium bowl; set aside.

Combine the potatoes with water to cover in a large saucepan. Cover and bring to a boil over medium-high heat. Reduce the heat to a simmer and cook until tender, 15 to 20 minutes.

Meanwhile, place the remaining 8 garlic cloves and remaining 2 tablespoons oil in a small skillet. Turn the heat to medium-low and cook the garlic, turning, until golden, about 5 minutes.

Drain the potatoes, reserving ¼ cup of the potato cooking water, and return the potatoes to the pot. Add the garlic and its oil, the cheese, and onion and mash with a fork, adding some of the reserved potato water if necessary, to make lumpy mashed potatoes. Cover and keep warm.

Wrap the pitas in foil and heat in the oven until warm, about 10 minutes.

To assemble, spread each pita with about 2 tablespoons of cucumber-yogurt sauce. Divide half the lettuce and tomatoes among the sandwiches and top each with one-fourth of the potato mixture. Divide the remaining yogurt sauce, lettuce, and tomatoes among the sandwiches. Wrap and serve.

Serves 4

eggs and potatoes, p.m. style

Most of us think eggs are for breakfast and potatoes are a side dish. In the vegetarian life, eggs are always on the table, and potatoes frequently star. Tossed with a little mayo (or olive oil), onion, and a few interesting flavorings, boiled eggs make a satisfying lunch. Paired with vegetables and cheese, eggs become a quick supper frittata. And soaked with milk and chewy French bread, eggs are the base for a hearty strata.

Potatoes—with your choice of 7 interesting fillings included—star in super-fast twice baked potatoes. And who needs leftover potatoes to make hash? Starting from scratch you can be sitting down to dinner in about 30 minutes.

Feel like eating these dishes in the morning? They're all pretty comfortable on the a.m. table too.

egg salad anytime

It's easy to turn tuna, chicken, seafood, or ham into a quick salad or sandwich, but if meat's not an option, what to do? Since most of us have at least a partial carton of eggs in the fridge, egg salad is an easy, satisfying alternative. And unlike some of their meatier counterparts, eggs are more neutrally flavored, making them open to so many flavoring possibilities.

Egg salad can be as simple as chopped eggs mixed with some kind of fat (olive oil or mayonnaise) and salt and pepper; but every exceptional salad usually has a little onion for kick and crunch, a little acid to perk things up, and flavorings to keep it interesting.

So using the basic recipe as a guide, pick a variation—there are seven in all. It'll tell you the fat to use, the onion to choose, and a set of distinct flavoring ingredients. You'll have enough variety to keep you going for a week and the knowledge to start creating your own signature salads.

master formula egg salad

6 large hard-boiled eggs, peeled and
   chopped (see Perfect Boiled Eggs,
   below)
¼ cup Fat
¼ cup minced Onion (Pick 1)
Extras (Pick 1 or 2)
Acids (Pick 1)
Herbs/Spices (Pick 1)
Salt and ground black pepper

Combine the eggs, Fat, Onion, Extras, Acid,
Herbs/Spices, and salt and pepper to taste in a
bowl. Mix well until combined.

Serves 4

perfect boiled eggs

6 large eggs

Place the eggs in a medium saucepan with
water to cover, making sure they fit in a single
layer. Cover the pan and bring to a full boil
over medium-high heat. Remove from the heat
and let stand, covered, for 10 minutes. Drain off
the water and run cold water over the eggs
until the saucepan has completely cooled. Add
1 quart of ice cubes to the water to cool the
eggs as quickly as possible.

Serves 6

egg salad options

Fat (Pick 1)

- Mayonnaise
- Olive oil

Onion (Pick 1)

- Sweet white onion
- Red onion
- Shallots
- Scallions

Extras (Pick 1 or 2)

- $\frac{1}{4}$ cup diced celery
- $\frac{1}{4}$ cup coarsely chopped Kalamata olives
- $\frac{1}{4}$ cup coarsely chopped cornichons
- $\frac{1}{4}$ cup diced oil-packed sun-dried tomatoes
- $\frac{1}{4}$ cup golden raisins
- 2 tablespoons capers, coarsely chopped
- 2 tablespoons pickle relish
- $\frac{1}{2}$ medium jalapeño, minced

Acids (Pick 1)

- 2 tablespoons horseradish
- $\frac{1}{4}$ cup salsa
- 1 tablespoon lemon juice
- 2 teaspoons lime juice or rice vinegar
- 2 teaspoons Dijon or spicy brown mustard

Herbs/Spices (Pick 1)

- 1 tablespoon chopped cilantro, dill, or parsley
- 2 teaspoons minced fresh oregano, tarragon, or thyme
- 1 teaspoon cumin or curry powder

pam's fave combos for egg salad

Olive oil, red onion, Kalamata, lemon juice, and oregano

Mayonnaise, shallots, cornichons, capers, Dijon mustard, and thyme

Olive oil, sweet white onion, minced jalapeño, salsa, lime juice, cilantro, and cumin

Mayonnaise, sweet white onion, celery, horseradish, and fresh dill

Mayonnaise, sweet white onion, golden raisins, celery, rice vinegar, cilantro, and curry powder

Mayonnaise, red onion, celery, sweet pickle relish, spicy brown mustard, and parsley

Olive oil, scallions, and oil-packed sun-dried tomatoes (since sun-dried tomatoes are acidic, no need for additional acid), and basil

frittatas on the fly

When you need dinner pronto, there's nothing much faster or more satisfying than a puffy, cheesy vegetable frittata.

For years I baked my frittatas. It's a fine method, but not long ago it occurred to me that if I just made them thinner, I could make them more quickly. Now I start them stovetop and then give them a quick puff under the broiler, shaving about 10 minutes off the total cooking time.

Since eggs and cheese are a given in a frittata, start by choosing a vegetable. It cooks right in the skillet you'll be cooking the frittata in.

Once your vegetable is prepped, it's like making an omelet. If you like, dollop on little spoonfuls of ricotta. Not only does it add low-fat creaminess, this lean cheese transforms your frittata from a light meal to a more substantial, satisfying dinner.

With decent knife skills and a little kitchen proficiency, you should be able to make a frittata—from prep to sliding it onto a cutting board—in about 15 minutes. Now that's a quick dinner.

master formula frittata on the fly

8 large eggs
Salt and ground black pepper
¼ cup grated Parmesan cheese
Heaping ½ cup **Additional Cheese**
(Pick 1)
Herbs (Pick 1; optional)
8 ounces **Vegetables** (Pick 1 or more)
1½ tablespoons olive oil
1 large garlic clove, minced
½ cup part-skim ricotta (optional,
but very nice)

Adjust an oven rack to the upper position and turn the broiler to high.

Season the eggs lightly with salt, pepper, Parmesan, **Additional Cheese,** and **Herb** (if using); set aside.

For **Tender Vegetables/Tender Greens,** heat the oil in a large (12-inch) ovenproof nonstick skillet over medium-high heat until shimmering. Add the vegetable(s) and cook, seasoning lightly with salt and pepper, until tender (or greens wilt), 2 to 5 minutes. Reduce the heat to medium, add the garlic, and cook for about 1 minute to blend the flavors.

For **Firm Vegetables/Sturdy Greens,** combine the oil, ⅓ cup water, the vegetable(s) of choice, a light sprinkling of salt and pepper, and the garlic in a large (12-inch) ovenproof nonstick skillet. Place the skillet over high heat, cover, and steam until the vegetable is bright and just tender (or until greens wilt), 4 to 5 minutes. Uncover and cook, stirring occasionally, until the liquid evaporates and the ingredients start to sauté.

Shake the skillet to distribute the vegetables evenly and add the egg mixture. Using a wooden spatula to push back eggs that have set, tilt the pan slightly so that uncooked eggs run into the empty portion of the pan. When the eggs start to set around the edges, remove from the heat. If using the optional ricotta, dollop it over the frittata. Broil the frittata until the eggs are puffed and spotty brown, 3 to 5 minutes.

Serves 4

frittata options

Additional Cheese (Pick 1)

- Crumbled goat cheese or feta
- Grated extra-sharp Cheddar, Gruyère, provolone, fontina, Swiss, pepper Jack

Herbs (Pick 1; optional)

- ½ teaspoon dried thyme leaves, oregano, or tarragon; or 1½ teaspoons minced fresh
- Generous ½ teaspoon dried dill weed or 2 teaspoons minced fresh dill
- 1 teaspoon dried basil or 2 tablespoons chopped fresh
- 1 tablespoon chopped fresh parsley or cilantro

Vegetables (Pick 1 or more. Each of the quantities below yields 8 ounces, so adjust quantities accordingly if using 2 or more, for 8 ounces total)

Tender Vegetables/Tender Greens

- Bell peppers (about 1 large)—stemmed, cored, and cut into short, thin strips
- Zucchini and yellow squash (about 2 medium-small)—halved lengthwise and thinly sliced
- Onions (about 1 medium-large)—halved from root to stem end and thinly sliced
- Leeks (2 medium-small)—white and light green parts only, quartered lengthwise, cut crosswise into ½-inch-thick slices, and thoroughly washed

- Sliced mushrooms (8-ounce package)—I prefer baby bellas (aka cremini) to whites; I think they have more flavor
- Fresh plum tomatoes (3 medium)—sliced medium-thick. (Don't use regular or cherry tomatoes because they have too much moisture.)
- Fennel (about 1 small bulb)—stalks and fronds discarded, bulb halved, cored, and thinly sliced crosswise
- Baby spinach or arugula—no prep—just add to hot oil and cook
- Beet greens and Swiss chard—thoroughly washed, stemmed, leaves coarsely chopped (about 8 cups)
- Frozen artichoke hearts (9-ounce box)—thawed and quartered, or a 14-ounce can, drained
- Frozen corn (half a 16-ounce package or one 10-ounce box)—thawed

Firm Vegetables/Sturdy Greens

- Asparagus (a trimmed 1-pound bunch of asparagus yields about 8 ounces)—tough ends snapped off, tips cut off, spears halved and cut into 1-inch lengths
- Broccoli crowns (2 heaping cups florets and stems)—cut into small florets
- Potatoes (about 4 small)—cut into small dice
- Winter squash—peeled, seeded, and cut into bite-size chunks
- Kale, collards, turnip greens—washed thoroughly, stemmed, and coarsely chopped (with these assertively flavored greens you may find 4 to 5 ounces sufficient)

pam's fave combos for frittata

Spinach (or zucchini), feta, and fresh dill

Potatoes, pepper Jack, and thyme

Kale, provolone, and oregano

Asparagus, Gruyère, and tarragon

Mushrooms, fontina, and thyme

Tomatoes, goat cheese, and tarragon

Leeks, sharp Cheddar, and parsley

notes and tips

- Sturdy greens like kale and firm vegetables—potatoes, broccoli, and asparagus—need steam/sautéing. For this method, place the vegetable and a little water, oil, and salt in a covered nonstick skillet over high heat. The small amount of seasoned water heats quickly, steams the vegetable, and then evaporates, at which point the oil kicks in and starts to sauté the vegetable. This is the moment to add the eggs. ➤

- For frittata for 2, you can halve the ingredients and switch to a medium (10-inch) nonstick skillet. But since frittatas reheat well in the microwave, you may want to make the bigger one. Leftovers make a great impromptu breakfast, light meal, or savory snack a day or two later.

- Take the frittata off the heat before the top is set; it should be appreciably wet when you dollop on the cheese and slide under the broiler. ➤

supper strata

Strata is the perfect main course for a large brunch. It's easy to prep ahead. It's sturdy, forgiving, and a real crowd-pleaser. The ingredients are readily available and pleasantly priced. But strata for supper? It's the instructions to "refrigerate overnight" that throw most of us off. In fact, strata doesn't need a night in the fridge to absorb the liquid. The milk and eggs soak into the bread almost as quickly as water into a sponge.

But to get strata on the table for dinner quickly and simply, you need a strategy. Start by heating the oven and microwaving the milk. Not only does the bread absorb hot milk faster, warm custard also sets more quickly in the oven.

While the milk heats, thinly slice the better part of a good baguette. Thinly sliced bread absorbs liquid more quickly. Thinner slices also means there are more of them to create a third layer so the cheese gets more evenly distributed.

After slowly whisking the hot milk into the beaten eggs, start the layering—two of bread, custard, and cheese with another round of bread and custard, reserving the final sprinkling of cheese for topping the vegetable. While you prep and cook the vegetable, the strata has plenty of time to absorb the custard.

Top the strata with a final layer of cheese and pop it in the oven. In 35 unattended minutes, you've got dinner. Leftover strata heats very well in the microwave, making it a perfect impromptu meal for later in the week.

master formula supper strata

2 cups whole milk
6 large eggs
Salt and ground black pepper
$\frac{1}{8}$ teaspoon ground nutmeg
1 good baguette (scant 1 pound), cut into
$\frac{1}{4}$- to $\frac{1}{3}$-inch-thick slices
8 ounces extra-sharp Cheddar cheese,
grated ($2\frac{1}{2}$ loosely packed cups)
$\frac{1}{4}$ cup thinly sliced scallions
$1\frac{1}{2}$ tablespoons olive oil
8 ounces Vegetables (Pick 1 or more)

Adjust an oven rack to the upper-middle position and preheat the oven to 350°F.

Meanwhile, place the milk in a glass measuring cup or other microwave-safe container and microwave until steamy hot.

Beat the eggs with $\frac{1}{2}$ teaspoon salt, several grinds of pepper, and the nutmeg until smooth. Whisk the hot milk into the eggs, slowly at first to prevent curdling, until smooth.

Make 2 layers in an 8-inch square baking pan in the following order: one-third each of the bread slices, milk mixture, cheese, and scallions. Make a third layer with the remaining bread and milk mixture. Set the remaining cheese and scallions aside. Lay a sheet of plastic wrap over the pan; set a salad plate and enough weight to submerge the bread without the milk overflowing the pan.

Heat the oil in a large skillet over medium-high heat. Add the Vegetable(s), sprinkle lightly with salt and pepper, and cook until crisp-tender, 3 to 4 minutes. Remove the plate and weights and spread the vegetables over the strata; top with the remaining cheese and scallions.

Bake until the custard just sets, about 35 minutes. Without adjusting the oven rack, turn on the broiler; broil until the strata is spotty brown and puffy, about 5 minutes.

Remove from the oven and let stand for 5 minutes before serving.

Serves 6

strata options

Vegetables (Pick 1 or more. Each of the quantities below yields 8 ounces, so adjust quantities accordingly if using 2 or more, for 8 ounces total)

- 8 ounces sliced mushrooms (preferably baby bellas, aka cremini)—diced
- 1 medium-large red onion—finely diced
- 1 medium-large bell pepper—stemmed, cored, and finely diced; a mix of colors looks especially nice
- 8 ounces thin to medium-thick asparagus spears (from 1 pound trimmed)—cut crosswise into small pieces
- 2 medium leeks—white and light green parts only, quartered lengthwise, finely diced, and thoroughly washed
- 8 ounces cherry tomatoes—halved and tossed with 1 tablespoon of oil (omit the remaining ½ tablespoon) along with a light sprinkling of salt and pepper. This is the only one that doesn't get cooked.

variation: orange cream cheese strata

1½ cups whole milk
6 ounces reduced-fat (Neufchâtel) cream cheese
1 tablespoon sugar
1 teaspoon finely grated orange zest and 2 tablespoons juice from a large orange
1 teaspoon vanilla extract
4 large eggs
1 good baguette, sliced about ¼- to ⅓-inch thick
¾ cup dried cranberries
¼ cup chopped walnuts
½ cup orange marmalade

Microwave the milk until steamy hot. With a hand mixer, beat the cream cheese, sugar, orange zest, and vanilla in a medium bowl, adding the eggs one at a time, to form a lumpy batter. Beat in the milk, slowly at first, to prevent curdling.

In an 8-inch square pan, layer in one-third each of the bread slices, milk mixture, and cranberries, in that order. Repeat twice more. Lay a sheet of plastic wrap over the pan; set a salad plate on top and weight to submerge the bread. Let stand for at least 15 minutes and up to 12 hours in the refrigerator.

Adjust the oven rack to the upper-middle position and preheat the oven to 350°F. Sprinkle the casserole with the walnuts, lightly pressing them into the bread. Bake until the casserole is firm and puffy, about 35 minutes.

Meanwhile, stir the marmalade and orange juice together in a small saucepan. Heat until warm and fluid.

Remove strata from oven, let stand 5 minutes. Cut into 6 portions and serve immediately with the orange sauce.

Serves 6

pam's fave combos for supper strata

Mushrooms and leeks

Asparagus alone

Leeks and asparagus

Leeks and mushrooms

Asparagus and mushrooms

Peppers and red onion

Cherry tomatoes

notes and tips

• The number of bread slices you need will depend on the size of the baguette. For the three layers in my 8-inch pan, I usually need about 45 thin slices from a long, thin baguette.

• For this, diced vegetables work best. Smaller pieces cook more quickly and the strata cuts better. Flavorful vegetables like red onions, leeks, asparagus, mushrooms, and peppers are all good choices, as are halved cherry tomatoes, which do not need to be pre-cooked at all—simply toss with oil and a light sprinkling of salt and pepper.

• If using leeks or red onion as the vegetable, you can (but don't have to) eliminate the scallions from the recipe. And although the vegetables add color and substance, plain cheese is nice once in a while.

• Thin-slicing the baguette helps the liquid absorb more quickly. ➤

• Heating the milk allows the custard to set faster. ➤

meatless hash

Funny how many people think hash is leftover meat and potatoes when you don't actually need either to make a fantastic hash. Better still, it's possible to make great meatless hash—from start to finish, no leftovers required—in less than 30 minutes.

The good news is that hash can be prepped ahead. It's also possible to almost completely cook the hash a couple of hours ahead. Store the cooked vegetable mixture in a bowl and spread the cooked potatoes on a large baking sheet, covering them with plastic wrap once they've cooled. About 10 minutes before you plan to serve, heat up the skillet, add the potatoes to re-crisp them, stir in the vegetable mixture and flavorings, and it's ready 5 minutes later.

Hash should be eaten hot off the stove. I've been known to warm up leftovers for lunch, but it's nothing I'd serve to company. Any of these hashes can be topped with a fried or poached egg or a dollop of light sour cream. A mix of purple, Yukon Gold, and russets makes an especially attractive hash.

master formula meatless hash

¼ cup vegetable or olive oil
1 pound **Vegetables** (Pick 1)
1 large onion, finely diced, or
1 medium-large onion and 1 small bell
pepper (any color), stemmed, cored,
and finely diced
Salt and ground black pepper
1½ pounds baking potatoes, cut into
¼-inch dice (about 5 cups)
2 tablespoons ketchup
1 tablespoon Dijon mustard
Dried Herbs/Spices (Pick 1, optional)
2 tablespoons **Fresh Herbs** (Pick 1,
optional)

Heat 2 tablespoons of the oil in a 12-inch nonstick skillet over low heat.

Meanwhile, cut up the **Vegetable** and onion (or onion and bell pepper). Two minutes or so before cooking, increase the heat to medium-high. When the oil starts to send up wisps of smoke, add the vegetable and cook, stirring occasionally, until golden, 5 to 7 minutes, depending on vegetable's moisture level. Add the onion (and pepper, if using), season lightly with salt and black pepper, and cook until the onion softens, about 5 minutes.

While the vegetables cook, dice the potatoes and toss with the remaining 2 tablespoons oil. Transfer the cooked vegetables to a baking sheet and set aside. Add the potatoes to the empty skillet and cook, stirring only occasionally so that they form a golden brown crust, about 10 minutes.

Meanwhile, mix the ketchup, mustard, 2 tablespoons of water, the **Dried Herb/Spice** (if using), and/or **Fresh Herb** (if using) in a cup.

Return the cooked vegetables to the skillet and stir in the ketchup mixture. Cook, stirring frequently, until the flavors meld and the hash has browned nicely, about 5 minutes.

Serves 4

hash options

Vegetable (Pick 1)

- Baby bellas (aka cremini) or white mushrooms—sliced
- Thawed frozen or fresh corn kernels (scant 3 cups/5 ears fresh)
- Brussels sprouts—trimmed and thinly sliced
- Eggplant—cut into $\frac{1}{4}$-inch dice
- Carrots—peeled and cut into $\frac{1}{4}$-inch dice
- White turnips or rutabaga (yellow turnips)—peeled and cut into $\frac{1}{4}$-inch dice
- Sweet potatoes—peeled and cut into $\frac{1}{4}$-inch dice
- Butternut squash—peeled, seeded, and cut into $\frac{1}{4}$-inch dice

Dried Herbs/Spices (Pick 1; optional)

- $\frac{1}{2}$ teaspoon dried thyme leaves
- $\frac{1}{2}$ teaspoon Italian seasoning
- $\frac{1}{2}$ teaspoon herbes de Provence
- 2 teaspoons sweet or hot paprika
- 1 teaspoon ground cumin

Fresh Herbs (Pick 1; optional)

- 3 tablespoons chopped parsley, basil, or cilantro
- 2 tablespoons chopped sage or dill

pam's fave combos for meatless hash

Mushrooms, dried thyme leaves, and fresh parsley

Onion-pepper combination, corn, cumin, and fresh cilantro

Rutabagas (yellow turnips) and fresh dill

Brussels sprouts and fresh sage

Onion-pepper combination, eggplant, Italian seasoning, and fresh basil (feel free to use more than the suggested amount of basil here)

Sweet potatoes, sweet or hot paprika, and fresh parsley

notes and tips

- When you are starting hash with raw ingredients, it helps to cook in batches. Give the flavoring vegetable a head start before adding the onions. Remove them from the skillet and then add the potatoes. With the skillet all to themselves, the potatoes can quickly brown and crisp. Return the cooked vegetables to the skillet for flavor blending and final browning and crisping. ➤

- If you want to get some of the chopping out of the way, prepare and measure all of the ingredients in advance, tossing the potatoes in 2 tablespoons of oil and covering them with plastic wrap. Any slight darkening will be masked in the cooking. Don't soak the diced potatoes in water. Although it keeps them from turning dark, it also prevents them from browning.

- So the potatoes don't stick, use a nonstick skillet.

- Hash needs a little liquid to bind it. Too much, however, and the dish stews and loses its crisp surfaces and bits. ➤

- For 2 servings, halve the ingredients and switch to a medium (10-inch) skillet.

super-fast twice baked potatoes

Who has time to bake even small potatoes—much less the jumbo twice baked variety—on a weeknight? Enter the microwave. While I don't like the leathery texture of fully microwaved potatoes, I wholeheartedly endorse the microwave for efficiently par-cooking them while the oven preheats. Just 8 minutes on high power and potatoes are piping hot, their flesh just starting to soften.

Another 30 minutes in the conventional oven is plenty of time for the flesh to turn soft and fluffy and skin to bake up irresistibly crisp. It also frees up time to make one of the full-flavored sauces that transform a plain tuber into a hearty, satisfying main course.

While the potatoes bake, make one of the sauces that follow. It's hard to choose—they're all very good. No need to wait long for the potatoes to cool. Holding them in a potholder or thick towel, you can split and scoop the flesh almost immediately. And since the potatoes are hot and the sauces are warm, they don't need much oven time the second round.

master formula super-fast twice baked potatoes

3 large baking potatoes (12 ounces each), washed and thoroughly dried and pricked
$\frac{1}{2}$ teaspoon olive oil
$\frac{1}{2}$ teaspoon kosher salt
Spud Sauce (Pick 1 from pages 195–196)
Ground black pepper

Adjust an oven rack to the middle position and preheat the oven to 400°F.

Rub the potatoes with the oil and salt and microwave for 8 minutes. When the oven is preheated, transfer the potatoes to a rimmed baking sheet and bake until tender, about 30 minutes.

Meanwhile, make the Spud Sauce you've chosen.

Let the potatoes cool slightly, then halve and scoop out the flesh into a medium bowl, leaving enough potato to form a sturdy shell. Toss the scooped potato with half of the Spud Sauce, seasoning to taste with salt and pepper. Divide the filling equally among the potato shells; top with the remaining sauce and bake until warmed through, about 12 minutes. Leaving the oven rack where it is, turn the oven to broil. Broil until golden brown, about 3 minutes.

Serves 4 to 6

mushroom-cream spud sauce with mustard and tarragon

¾ cup good-quality vegetable broth
¾ cup evaporated milk (2% or regular)
1 tablespoon Dijon mustard
3 tablespoons olive oil
1 pound sliced cremini mushrooms
Salt and ground black pepper
3 large garlic cloves, minced
1 teaspoon dried tarragon
2 tablespoons all-purpose flour
⅓ cup grated Parmesan cheese
2 tablespoons thinly sliced scallion greens, for garnish

Combine the broth, evaporated milk, and mustard in a 1-quart glass measuring cup and microwave until steamy, 3 to 4 minutes.

Meanwhile, heat 2 tablespoons of the oil in a large skillet over medium-high heat. Add the mushrooms and cook until their liquid evaporates and the mushrooms are golden brown, stirring infrequently at first and seasoning lightly with salt and pepper at the end, 6 to 7 minutes. Add the garlic and tarragon and cook until fragrant, 1 to 2 minutes. Transfer to a medium bowl.

Add the remaining 1 tablespoon oil to the empty skillet. Whisk in the flour, and then the hot milk mixture, simmering over medium-high heat until the sauce thickens, about 1 minute. Whisk in the Parmesan and then stir the mushroom mixture back into the sauce.

Assemble and bake the potatoes as described in the Master Formula, sprinkling the scallions over the stuffed and sauced potatoes before baking.

spinach-feta spud sauce with scallions and dill

2 packages (10 ounces each) frozen chopped spinach, thawed
¾ cup evaporated milk (2% or regular)
2 tablespoons olive oil
3 large garlic cloves, minced
2 tablespoons all-purpose flour
¼ cup chopped fresh dill
2 thinly sliced scallions
¾ cup crumbled feta cheese
Salt and ground black pepper

Squeeze the thawed spinach over a measuring cup and mix ¾ cup of the spinach juice with the evaporated milk in a 1-quart glass measuring cup or other microwave-safe container. Microwave until steamy hot, 3 to 4 minutes.

Meanwhile, combine the oil and garlic in a large skillet. Turn the heat to medium-high and cook until the garlic starts to sizzle. Whisk in the flour and hot milk mixture and simmer

(continued)

until the sauce thickens, about 1 minute. Stir in the spinach, dill, and scallions and cook, stirring constantly, until the mixture starts to cling to the pan bottom, 1 to 2 minutes.

Remove from the heat and stir in $\frac{1}{2}$ cup of the feta. Adjust the seasonings, including salt and pepper to taste.

Assemble and bake the potatoes as described in the Master Formula, sprinkling the stuffed and sauced potatoes with the remaining $\frac{1}{4}$ cup of feta before baking.

pissaladière spud sauce with gruyère

¾ cup good-quality vegetable broth
¾ cup evaporated milk (2% or regular)
3 tablespoons olive oil
1 pound onions (2 medium-large), halved and thinly sliced
Salt and ground black pepper
3 large garlic cloves, minced
1 teaspoon dried thyme leaves
2 tablespoons all-purpose flour
½ cup pitted olives, coarsely chopped
½ cup grated Gruyère cheese

Combine the broth and evaporated milk in a 1-quart glass measuring cup or other microwave-safe container until steamy, 3 to 4 minutes.

Meanwhile, heat 2 tablespoons of the oil in a large skillet over medium-high heat. Add the onions and cook until caramel brown, stirring infrequently at first and seasoning lightly with salt and pepper at the end, 8 to 10 minutes.

Add the garlic and thyme and cook until fragrant, 1 to 2 minutes. Transfer to a medium bowl.

Add the remaining 1 tablespoon oil to the empty skillet. Whisk in the flour, and then the hot milk mixture, simmering over medium-high heat until the sauce thickens, about 1 minute. Stir the onion mixture into the sauce.

Assemble and bake the potatoes as described in the Master Formula, sprinkling the stuffed and sauced potatoes with the olives and cheese before baking.

samosa spud sauce

1½ cups good-quality vegetable broth
4 tablespoons butter
1 pound onions (2 medium-large), halved and thinly sliced
Salt and ground black pepper
1 tablespoon minced garlic
1 tablespoon minced fresh ginger
1 cup frozen green peas, thawed
1 teaspoon ground cumin
1 teaspoon ground coriander
1 teaspoon turmeric
2 tablespoons all-purpose flour

Place the broth in a 1-quart glass measuring cup and microwave until steamy, about 2 minutes.

Heat 2 tablespoons of the butter in a large skillet over medium-high heat. Add the onions and cook until caramel brown, stirring infrequently at first and seasoning lightly with salt and pepper at the end, 8 to 10 minutes.

Add the garlic and ginger and cook until fragrant, 1 to 2 minutes. Transfer to a medium bowl. Stir in the peas.

Add the remaining 2 tablespoons butter and the spices to the empty skillet and cook until fragrant. Whisk in the flour and then the hot broth, and simmer over medium-high heat until the sauce thickens, 1 to 2 minutes. Stir the onion mixture into the sauce.

Assemble and bake the potatoes as described in the Master Formula.

Note: Garnish with a little chopped fresh cilantro and serve with Major Grey's or other chutney. If you want a little heat, add minced fresh jalapeño along with the garlic and ginger.

notes and tips

- Although the skin isn't as crisp, these potatoes are excellent reheated in the microwave or oven. Or do a little of both—use the microwave to take the chill off and finish them in the oven. However they get reheated, they're thrice baked now!

- Rubbing the potatoes with oil and coarse salt makes the skin more flavorful (and more likely to be eaten). ➤

- Leave a thick enough shell to hold its shape once the filling is spooned in. ➤

pie for dinner

Whether it's pot pie, pizza pie, a French galette, or quiche, most of us don't think these kinds of satisfying comfort dishes are possible from scratch on a weeknight. With a little store-bought dough or pastry and a little formula in your head, you can pull these off most any night, most any season.

vegetable pot pies

Used to be that pot pie was a weekend dish. It was too time-consuming to make during the week. With my method, pot pie is possible anytime you've got 50 minutes (20 of which is oven time, which means free time for you).

The technique for cooking pot pie starts with choosing and preparing the vegetables. Then set the pan in the oven, turn on the heat, and let the preheating oven cook them while you prepare the rest of the dish.

Then make a quick béchamel and add it to the cooked vegetables as they emerge from the oven. Pour the mixture into a deep-dish pie pan. Cover it with the refrigerated pie crust. Flute it, if you like.

Since the sauce and vegetables are fully cooked and hot, the pie needs only enough baking time for the pastry to turn golden brown, which should be about 25 to 30 minutes.

It's Monday night, and maybe that means meatless for you. Bring this piping hot to the table and they'll swear it's Sunday supper.

master formula vegetable pot pie

Onion (Pick 1)
1 pound Potatoes (Pick 1)
1 pound Vegetables (Pick at least 2 or 3)
4 tablespoons olive oil
¾ teaspoon Dried Herbs (Pick 1)
Salt and ground black pepper
1 cup good-quality vegetable broth
1 cup evaporated milk (2% or regular)
¼ cup all-purpose flour
3 tablespoons dry sherry
¼ cup grated Parmesan cheese
¼ cup frozen peas
One 9-inch refrigerated pie crust
(from a 14.1-ounce package)

Toss the Onion, Potatoes, and Vegetables with 2 tablespoons of the oil, ½ teaspoon of the Dried Herb, and a generous sprinkling of salt and pepper in a 9 x 13-inch pan. Adjust an oven rack to the lowest position and place the pan on the rack. Turn the oven to 425°F and roast the vegetables until tender, stirring occasionally, about 20 minutes. Remove the vegetables from the oven but leave the oven on and leave the rack at the lowest position.

Meanwhile, combine the broth and evaporated milk in a 1-quart glass measuring cup or other microwave-safe container until steamy, 3 to 4 minutes. Heat the remaining 2 tablespoons oil in a large saucepan or Dutch oven over medium heat. Whisk in the flour and the remaining ¼ teaspoon herb; cook until golden, about 1 minute. Whisk in the milk mixture and cook, whisking, until the sauce comes to a boil and fully thickens. Stir in the sherry and Parmesan, and season to taste with salt and pepper.

Add the sauce to the cooked vegetables along with the peas; adjust the seasonings.

Pour the mixture into a 9-inch deep-dish pie plate. Cover the filling with the pie crust and flute as desired. Depending on the pie plate design, you may have to roll it into a slightly larger round. Bake until the sauce is bubbling and the crust is golden brown, 25 to 30 minutes. Let cool slightly before serving.

Serves 4 to 6

pot pie options

Onion (Pick 1)

- Large red onion—cut into medium dice
- Large white onion—cut into medium dice
- Medium leek—white and light green part only, quartered lengthwise, cut into medium dice, and well washed

Potatoes (Pick 1)

- Red potatoes—cut into medium dice
- Sweet potatoes—peeled and cut into medium dice
- Yukon Golds—peeled and cut into medium dice

Vegetables (Pick at least 2 or 3)

- Cabbage—quartered, cored, and cut into short $1/2$-inch-square pieces
- Cauliflower—cut into small florets
- Asparagus (start with 1 pound, which yields 8 ounces once the tough ends are snapped off)—spears cut into $1/2$-inch lengths
- Winter squash—peeled, seeded, and cut into small dice
- Carrots—peeled and cut into $1/2$-inch-thick slices
- Celery—cut into $1/2$-inch-thick slices
- Turnips—peeled and cut into small dice
- Rutabagas (yellow turnips)—peeled, quartered, and cut into small dice
- Baby bella (aka cremini) mushrooms—sliced

Dried Herbs (Pick 1)

- Thyme
- Tarragon
- Basil

pam's fave combos for pot pies

Red onion, ½ pound each cremini mushrooms and chopped cabbage (about ¼ small head), red boiling or sweet potatoes, and thyme

Leeks, 2 carrots, 2 celery ribs, ½ pound cremini mushrooms, red potatoes, and tarragon

Onion, cauliflower, carrots, red potatoes, and basil

Leeks, asparagus, carrots, and tarragon

Red onion, winter squash, turnips, and thyme

notes and tips

• Combine the veggies with the béchamel in the pan they roasted in, then transfer to the pie pan. ➤

• The white sauce I use throughout this book is both exceedingly rich and creamy *and* incredibly light and flavorful. With a classic white sauce, or béchamel, the usual ratio of butter to flour is 1:1. To cut back on calories I reduce the fat by half—a 1:2 ratio. It's the smallest amount necessary to thicken, yet it still gives the sauce wonderful flavor.

• Fluting the crust, though not essential, gives the pot pie an attractive, finished appearance. Pinch the dough from the outside edge and press into the V of your fingers with the point of your forefinger. ➤

• Classic white sauce is also typically made with milk, making the sauce taste one-dimensional. Instead I use evaporated milk, replacing the water that's been evaporated with more flavorful vegetable broth. I further enhance the sauce's flavor by stirring the Parmesan cheese into the thickened sauce.

week-night quiche

It took some effort to streamline this process, but the resulting quiche has it all: A crisp, golden bottom crust. A light, silky custard. A totally legit yet effortless crust. If you start with thawed pastry, you can turn out an elegant brunch, lunch, or supper main course—start to finish—in less than 45 minutes.

It all starts with a sheet of puff pastry and a preheating oven. Roll out the sheet to fit a 10 x 15-inch jelly-roll pan, pricking it to prevent puffing, and use fork tines to stamp it around the perimeter.

Next, choose one of the suggested vegetables, tossing it with oil, salt, and pepper. Salt seasons, but it also causes the vegetable to start releasing its liquid. For this reason, you'll want to get the pastry in the oven as soon as possible to prevent it from becoming soggy.

While the pastry bakes, prepare the custard. Heating the milk for your custard mixture takes the chill off, helping it set a little faster in the oven.

Once you've poured the custard over the vegetable, return the filled pastry to the oven. To gently bake the custard and lightly brown the pastry, lower the oven temperature and set the quiche on the upper-middle oven rack for warm, enveloping heat.

master formula week-night quiche

1 sheet (half a 17.3-ounce box) frozen
puff pastry, thawed
About 2 cups Vegetables
(Pick 1 or more)
1 tablespoon olive oil
Salt and ground black pepper
3 large eggs
Herbs/Spices/Aromatics (Pick 1, optional)
$\frac{1}{2}$ cup reduced-fat sour cream
$\frac{3}{4}$ cup evaporated milk, heated to
piping hot
$1\frac{1}{2}$ cups Cheese (Pick 1)

Adjust the oven racks to the lowest and upper-middle positions and preheat the oven to 400°F.

Roll the puff pastry on a lightly floured surface to a 16 x 11-inch rectangle. Fit into a 15 x 10-inch jelly-roll pan, making sure the pastry is not stretched; trim any overhang and prick the pastry all over with a fork.

Toss the Vegetable(s) with the oil and a light sprinkling of salt and pepper, then scatter evenly over the pastry, making sure they're in a single layer. Bake on the *lowest* oven rack until golden brown, 12 to 20 minutes (depending on where your oven's heating element is).

Meanwhile, whisk the eggs, a heaping $\frac{1}{4}$ teaspoon salt, several grinds of pepper, Herb/Spice/Aromatic (if using), and the sour cream. Slowly whisk in the hot evaporated milk.

Pour the egg mixture evenly over vegetables and sprinkle with Cheese. Transfer the pan to the upper rack, reduce the oven temperature to 300°F, and bake until the filling is just set, 20 to 25 minutes. Leaving the quiche in place, turn on the broiler and broil until the cheese bubbles, about 2 minutes. Let rest a couple of minutes before cutting and serving.

Serves 8

quiche options

Vegetables (Pick 1 or more. Each of the quantities below yields 2 cups, so adjust quantities accordingly if using 2 or more, for 2 cups total—enough to cover the pastry bottom without overcrowding it)

- **Sliced mushrooms (an 8-ounce container)**—factory-sliced mushrooms are convenient but a little thick for this quiche. Slice the thicker pieces and then halve them.
- **Cherry or grape tomatoes (about a pint)—halved.** Be sure to arrange them cut-side up on the pastry.
- **Thin asparagus (1-pound bunch)**—tough ends snapped off (no need to cut)
- **Red pepper–corn combo**—mix 1 cup diced pepper and 1 cup thawed frozen corn
- **Leeks (2 medium)**—white and light green parts only, quartered lengthwise, finely diced, and well washed
- **Frozen spinach**—(two 10-ounce boxes)—thawed, squeezed dry, and fluffed up

Herbs/Spices/Aromatics (Pick 1; optional, but nice)

- $\frac{1}{4}$ cup chopped fresh basil leaves or 1 teaspoon dried
- $\frac{1}{4}$ cup thinly sliced scallions
- 2 tablespoons chopped fresh parsley leaves
- $1\frac{1}{2}$ teaspoons minced fresh tarragon or $\frac{1}{2}$ teaspoon dried
- $1\frac{1}{2}$ teaspoons minced fresh thyme leaves or $\frac{1}{2}$ teaspoon dried
- Pinch of nutmeg

Cheese (Pick 1)

- Sharp Cheddar, grated
- Mozzarella, grated
- Provolone, grated
- Goat cheese, crumbled
- Mild Swiss or more assertive Gruyère, grated
- Pepper Jack, grated

pam's fave combos for weeknight quiche

Mushrooms, Gruyère, and thyme

Spinach, Swiss, and nutmeg

Leeks, goat cheese, and parsley

Tomato, mozzarella, and basil (fresh or dried)

Asparagus, Swiss, and tarragon

Pepper-corn combo, pepper Jack, and scallions

notes and tips

- If you forgot to thaw the pastry, don't worry. Microwaving it for 15 seconds dramatically speeds the process.

- Use scissors to cut the dough to size, allowing just enough to overlap the rim of the pan slightly. Pricking the crust very thoroughly keeps it from puffing and bubbling. Use the tines of a fork to crimp the edges and prevent the crust from shrinking down the sides. ➤

- During the first baking phase, the vegetables par-cook at the same time as the pastry browns, weighing it down as pie weights would. Even pricked pastry tends to puff, but the weight of the cooking vegetables mostly prevents it. Keep your eye on it, however. You may need to reach in and deflate the puffing pastry with the point of a sharp knife or the tines of a fork.

- To ensure that the bottom of the pastry browns well, it gets baked on the bottom oven rack. The baking time will depend on whether your heating element is located above or below the oven floor. I've found the above-floor heating elements brown the pastry much more quickly, so it could take as little as 12 minutes, and if your heating element is hidden below the floor, up to 20 minutes.

roasted vegetable galettes

I love the simplicity of these free-form vegetable tarts, known as galettes. Grab an onion, open the fridge, and check out your vegetable bin. There are plenty of options. Cut up enough vegetables (about 6 cups) so that with the onion there's enough to fill a large rimmed baking sheet in a single layer. Toss the vegetables with oil, salt, pepper, and a dried herb from the pantry (or maybe sprinkle on something from your fresh herb stash after the vegetables emerge from the oven).

As you slide the vegetables onto the bottom oven rack, hit 425°F and let the preheating oven cook them to perfection as you roll out pie pastry (if it's from the refrigerated case, just unfurl and roll a few inches more). Toss hot-out-of-the-oven vegetables with cheeses (your choice) plus cream cheese (or goat for a little edge), which enrich, bind, and flavor. Spread the mixture onto the pastry and fold up the sides. The oven's already hot, so just shove it in!

While the galette bakes, make a quick salad. There may be time to eat it as a first course, but in just 20 minutes you'll pull a beautiful, fragrant roasted-vegetable-and-cheese galette from the oven. It's hard to believe something so beautiful and delicious could be ready in 50 minutes flat.

master formula roasted vegetable galette

6 heaping cups Vegetables
(Pick 1 or more)
Onion (Pick 1)
2 tablespoons olive oil
Salt and ground black pepper
Dried/Fresh Herbs (Pick 1)
One 9-inch refrigerated pie crust
(from a 14.1-ounce package)
1 heaping cup Cheese (Pick 1)
4 ounces crumbled goat cheese
or light cream cheese

Toss the Vegetable(s), Onion, oil, a generous sprinkling of salt and pepper, and the Dried Herb (if using fresh, add it later) on a large rimmed baking sheet. Adjust the oven racks to the lowest and middle positions. Set the vegetables on the bottom rack in the cold oven and set the oven to 425°F. Roast, stirring once, until just cooked and starting to color, 15 to 20 minutes.

Meanwhile, roll the pie dough into a 14-inch circle and place on a large baking sheet. Mix three-fourths of the Cheese with the goat or cream cheese in a large bowl.

Add the hot vegetables (and the Fresh Herb, if using) to the cheese mixture and toss to thoroughly mix. Adjust the seasonings. Spread the mixture over the pastry, leaving a 2-inch border. Fold the 2-inch border in over the vegetables and sprinkle the filling with the remaining cheese. Bake on the middle rack until bubbling and golden brown, about 20 minutes. Let cool for 5 minutes before slicing and serving.

Serves 6

galette options

Vegetables (Pick 1 or more)

- Cabbage—quartered, cored, and cut into ½-inch-thick slices
- Small red, yellow, and/or purple potatoes—cut into ½-inch-thick slices
- Sweet potatoes—cut into ½-inch-thick slices
- Cauliflower—cut into small florets
- Asparagus—tough ends snapped off, cut into 1-inch lengths
- Winter squash—peeled, seeded, and cut into ½-inch-thick slices
- Carrots—peeled and cut into ½-inch-thick slices
- Turnips—peeled, halved, and cut into ½-inch-thick slices
- Rutabagas (yellow turnips)—peeled, quartered, and cut into ½-inch-thick slices
- Cherry or grape tomatoes—left whole
- Sliced cremini mushrooms
- Eggplant—quartered lengthwise and cut crosswise into ½-inch-thick slices (if using small Japanese eggplant, simply cut into ½-inch-thick slices)
- Zucchini or yellow squash—halved lengthwise and cut crosswise into ½-inch-thick slices (if using small zucchini, simply cut into ½-inch-thick slices)

Onion (Pick 1)

- 1 large red onion, halved and cut into ½-inch-thick slices
- 1 large yellow onion, halved and cut into ½-inch-thick slices
- 1 medium leek, white and light green part only, quartered lengthwise, cut into medium dice, and well washed

Dried/Fresh Herbs (Pick 1)

- 1 generous teaspoon dried thyme leaves, tarragon, dill weed, basil, herbes de Provence, Italian seasoning
- 1 teaspoon chopped fresh rosemary
- 1 tablespoon chopped fresh thyme leaves, tarragon, or dill
- ¼ cup chopped fresh basil

Cheese (Pick 1)

- Extra-sharp Cheddar, grated
- Mozzarella, grated
- Swiss, grated
- Gruyère, grated
- Fontina, grated
- Parmesan, grated

variation: spinach artichoke filling

Here is a galette filling variation that cooks on the stovetop. Prepare the filling, then proceed exactly as for Roasted Vegetable Galette. Canned artichoke hearts can sub for frozen.

2 tablespoons olive oil
1 medium leek, white and light green parts only, quartered lengthwise, cut into medium dice, and well washed
2 boxes (10 ounces) frozen chopped spinach, thawed and squeezed dry
1 box (9 ounces) frozen artichoke hearts, thawed
Salt and ground black pepper
1 tablespoon chopped fresh dill
½ cup grated Parmesan cheese
½ cup grated Swiss cheese
4 ounces cream cheese

Heat the oil in a large skillet over medium-high heat. Add the leek and cook until tender, 4 to 5 minutes. Add the spinach and artichoke hearts, seasoning to taste with salt and pepper, and cook until excess moisture evaporates. Stir in the dill. Transfer the mixture to a large bowl.

In a small bowl, combine the Parmesan and Swiss cheese. Stir three-fourths of this mixture and the cream cheese into the spinach mixture, tossing to coat.

Fill, form, and bake the galette as directed.

Serves 6

pam's fave combos for roasted vegetable galettes

Small potatoes, sweet potatoes, herbes de Provence, and Cheddar

Cabbage, butternut squash, dried or fresh thyme, and Gruyère

Eggplant, zucchini, cherry tomatoes, dried or fresh basil, and mozzarella and/or Parmesan

Asparagus, potatoes, dried or fresh tarragon, and fontina

notes and tips

- Unfurl the refrigerated pie crust onto a floured surface and roll fairly thin to enlarge from 10 inches in diameter to a 14-inch circle. ➤

- Mound the filling onto the center of the dough circle, then fold the edges up and over at 2- or 3-inch intervals, leaving the center open. Finish by sprinkling on the remaining cheese. ➤

roasted vegetable galettes | 217

simple (and simplest) veggie pizzas

If our local pizza shop relied on me for orders, they'd be out of business. That's because I've got a successful strategy for serving pizza any night of the week. If I've got a few minutes to make dough in the afternoon (it really is just 10 minutes in the food processor), I spread the word it's pizza night. We might download a movie we've been dying to watch or make it a fun evening around the kitchen island, but homemade pizza is always special. This is Simple Pizza.

Of course, there are always those days when even 18 minutes of advance planning isn't in the cards. For those nights I make it even simpler, with store-bought dough. If they didn't know better, everyone would be just as impressed as if I'd made pizzas from scratch.

And then there's Simplest Pizza: I always keep a few good-quality pre-baked thin pizza crusts in the freezer for nights David wants to cook or I just need to bang it out. They're ridiculously simple and quite good, and since you get to top them yourself, they're better for you than the greasy stuff that arrives in a cardboard box.

With these strategies and three no-cook pizza sauces and veggie toppings—no precooking required—you can finally throw out your take-out menus.

master formula simple veggie pizza

½ recipe Simple Pizza Dough (opposite) or 1-pound bag store-bought pizza dough
Sauce (Pick 1)
2 cups Vegetables (Pick 1 or more)
2 teaspoons oil
Salt and ground black pepper
Generous 1 cup grated pizza cheese (e.g., mozzarella/provolone blend)
¼ cup grated Parmesan cheese
Dried oregano
Red pepper flakes

Adjust the oven rack to the lowest position (if you have unglazed quarry tiles, line the oven rack with them) and preheat to 500°F.

Cut the dough into quarters and stretch each piece to a 12 x 4-inch rectangle. Place them crosswise on a large cornmeal-coated baking sheet.

Spread the Sauce over the pizzas. Toss the Vegetables with the oil and a light sprinkling of salt and pepper. Scatter over the sauce.

Bake until golden brown, 12 to 15 minutes. Top with pizza cheese; return to oven and bake until crisp and spotty brown, 5 minutes longer.

Sprinkle pizzas with Parmesan cheese and oregano and red pepper flakes to taste.

Serves 4

veggie pizza options

Sauce (Pick 1)

- No-Cook Red Sauce—Mix 1 cup crushed tomatoes with 1 large minced garlic clove and 1 tablespoon extra-virgin olive oil.

- No-Cook White Sauce—Mix 1 cup part-skim ricotta, 2 tablespoons milk, 2 large minced garlic cloves, and a generous sprinkling of salt and pepper.

- Pesto Sauce—Mix $\frac{1}{2}$ cup each part-skim ricotta and prepared pesto.

Vegetables (Pick 1 or more)

- Bell pepper (any color)—stemmed, cored, and cut into short, thin strips

- Red onion—quartered and cut into short, thin slices

- Mushrooms—cut into small dice

- Broccoli florets—cut into small pieces

- Grape or cherry tomatoes—halved and lightly salted. Don't choose these if you're topping the pizza with No-Cook Red Sauce.

- Eggplant—cut into small dice

- Zucchini—quartered lengthwise and thinly sliced crosswise

- Small red potatoes or fingerlings—thinly sliced

- Frozen chopped spinach—thawed and squeezed dry

simple pizza dough

$\frac{1}{2}$ cup warm water and $1\frac{1}{4}$ cups tepid water
1 envelope active dry yeast (or a generous 2 teaspoons)
2 tablespoons extra-virgin olive oil
4 cups bread flour
2 teaspoons table salt

Place the $\frac{1}{2}$ cup warm water in a 2-cup measuring cup. Whisk the yeast into the water and let stand until it dissolves and expands, about 5 minutes. Add the remaining $1\frac{1}{4}$ cups water and the oil to the yeast mixture.

Meanwhile, pulse the flour and salt in a large food processor fitted with a steel blade. Pour the yeast mixture over the flour and pulse to form a rough, soft ball. Continue to process until the dough is smooth and satiny, about 30 seconds longer. Turn the dough onto a floured work surface and knead a few seconds to form a smooth ball. Place in a bowl coated with cooking spray and cover with plastic wrap. Let rise until doubled in size, 2 to 3 hours.

Without punching it down, dump the dough onto a lightly floured work surface. Using a chef's knife or a metal dough scraper, halve the dough. Use one-half in the pizza recipe, stretching and shaping as directed. Punch down the remaining half and wrap and refrigerate or freeze for another time. Depending on your schedule, frozen dough can be thawed in the refrigerator or at room temperature.

Makes a scant 2 pounds or 8 small pizzas

variation: simplest veggie pizza

1 large (11- to 12-inch) thin-crust store-bought
   pizza crust
Sauce (Pick 1)
2 cups Vegetables (Pick 1 or more)
2 teaspoons oil
Salt and ground black pepper
Generous 1 cup grated pizza cheese
   (e.g., mozzarella/provolone blend)
¼ cup grated Parmesan cheese
Dried oregano
Red pepper flakes

Adjust the rack to the lower-middle position
and preheat to 450°F. Place the pizza crust on a
baking sheet or pizza pan.

Spread the Sauce over the pizza. Toss the
Vegetables with the oil and a light sprinkling
of salt and pepper. Scatter over the sauce.
Top the vegetables with pizza cheese first,
then bake until crisp and spotty brown, 12 to
15 minutes.

Sprinkle pizza with Parmesan cheese and
oregano and red pepper flakes to taste.

Serves 4

pam's fave combos for veggie pizzas

No-Cook White Sauce, peppers, and red
onion

Pesto Sauce and broccoli

No-Cook White Sauce and cherry tomatoes

No-Cook Red Sauce and eggplant

No-Cook White Sauce and potato

No-Cook Red Sauce and mushrooms

No-Cook White Sauce and red onion

Pesto Sauce and spinach

notes and tips

- Portion the dough and stretch each portion
  by hand into an oblong shape for easier
  baking and cutting. ➤

- Adding the cheese to the partially baked
  pizza ensures it won't dry out before the
  dough is completely cooked through. ➤

fast-food favorites: italian, asian, mexican

If you took a poll, Italian, Asian, and Mexican foods, in varying orders, would top just about everyone's list of favorite dining-out options. These foods also happen to adapt very readily to meatless menus, whether by substituting tofu, legumes, or eggplant in recipes that traditionally call for ground beef, sliced chicken, or pork or simply by upping the veggie quotient.

Pasta and risotto are weekly staples of my dinner repertoire (as are the warmed-up leftovers for lunch the next day). If that's true for you too, I'm guessing these next several pages will quickly become well worn. You'll also find formulas to satisfy the Asian addicts in your crew. We've all become accustomed to eating our pad Thai, lo mein, and fried rice out of a take-out container—but wouldn't it be better if the vegetables weren't wilted from their car ride and you knew exactly how much oil went into the wok beforehand?

And when it comes to fun food, Mexican dishes are my go-tos; quesadillas and tacos are some of the friendliest dishes around. Because beans and vegetables are the usual fillers here, it's an easy place to start weaning everyone off of meat.

supper pasta formulas: red white green

If you could have only one thing to eat for the rest of your life, what would it be? At our house we never seem to tire of that question, and invariably my answer is pasta. In this section I offer five very different pasta sauce formulas to which you can add vegetables and flavorings of your choice—enough variety to last a lifetime.

Each sauce is prepared slightly differently, which in turn affects how the vegetables are cooked, but the game plan remains the same. Start by choosing your sauce: your options include a light and creamy tomato sauce, a light Alfredo sauce, a white wine sauce, a creamy ricotta sauce, and a classic pesto. Pick the one that complements the season, the weather, or the wine you want to serve or that just suits your fancy.

Next, it's time to pick a vegetable. Firm vegetables and sturdy greens like broccoli, cauliflower, carrots, and kale cook very efficiently right in with the pasta. Tender vegetables like leeks, peppers, mushrooms, and zucchini are moist enough that a little olive oil and a hot pan are all they need to get tender. Simply sauté them and cook right in the sauce.

Since Creamy Ricotta Sauce and Presto Pesto are both uncooked and therefore don't require a second pan, tender vegetables make less sense with these sauces, but there's certainly nothing wrong with firing up a skillet and sautéing mushrooms to toss with Creamy Ricotta Sauce.

master formula veggie pasta with creamy tomato sauce

Bring 2 quarts of water and 1 tablespoon salt to a boil in a large soup kettle. Add the pasta and, using back-of-the-box times as a guide, cook, partially covered and stirring frequently at first to prevent sticking, until just tender. If using **Firm Vegetables/Sturdy Greens,** add to the boiling pasta water for the last 5 or so minutes of cooking. Drain and return to the pot along with the pasta.

Meanwhile, heat the oil in a large skillet over medium-high heat. If using **Tender Vegetables,** add them now and cook until crisp-tender, 5 to 7 minutes. Add the garlic and pepper flakes and cook until fragrant and golden, about 1 minute. (If not using tender vegetables, simply heat the garlic and pepper flakes with the oil.) Add the wine and bring to a simmer. Add the tomatoes, return to a simmer, and stir in the baking soda. Reduce the heat to medium-low and simmer until thick, 10 to 12 minutes.

Add the evaporated milk and **Fresh Herbs** if using and simmer for 3 to 4 minutes to blend the flavors. Add the sauce and $1/4$ cup of Parmesan to the drained pasta, tossing to coat. Adjust the seasonings. Serve sprinkled with additional Parmesan.

Serves 4

Salt
12 ounces pasta (bite-size, linguine, fettuccine, or spaghetti)
1 to $1^{1/2}$ pounds Vegetables (Pick 1 or more)
2 tablespoons olive oil
3 large garlic cloves, minced
$1/2$ teaspoon red pepper flakes
$1/2$ cup dry white wine
1 can (28 ounces) crushed tomatoes
$1/4$ teaspoon baking soda
1 cup evaporated milk
Fresh Herbs (optional)
$1/4$ cup Parmesan cheese, plus extra for topping

veggie pasta options

Vegetables (Pick 1 or more)

Firm Vegetables/Sturdy Greens

- Asparagus—tough stalks snapped off, cut into 1-inch lengths
- Snow peas or sugar snap peas—strings removed, if necessary
- Fresh or frozen green peas—figure no more than 1 cup and use with a mix of vegetables
- Broccoli or cauliflower—cut into small florets
- Carrots—peeled and thinly sliced
- White turnips or rutabaga (yellow turnip)—peeled and cut into small dice
- Butternut or other winter squash—peeled and cut into small dice
- Thin green beans—cut into 1½-inch lengths
- Spinach—stemmed if needed
- Bok choy—cored and thinly sliced crosswise
- Beet greens, Swiss chard, kale, collards, turnip greens—well washed, stemmed, and coarsely chopped

Tender Vegetables

- Zucchini or yellow squash—quartered lengthwise and cut into bite-size chunks
- Sliced white or baby bella (aka cremini) mushrooms
- Bell peppers—stemmed, cored, and thinly sliced
- Eggplant—quartered lengthwise and thinly sliced crosswise
- Fennel—stalks discarded, bulb halved, cored, and thinly sliced
- Cabbage—quartered, cored, and thinly sliced
- Onions (red, white, or yellow)—halved and thinly sliced crosswise
- Leeks—white and light green parts only, quartered lengthwise, cut into medium dice, and well washed

Fresh Herbs

- ¼ cup chopped parsley or basil
- 1½ to 2 teaspoons minced thyme, oregano, sage, or rosemary

master formula veggie pasta with light alfredo

Salt
12 ounces pasta (bite-size, linguine, fettuccine, or spaghetti)
1 to 1½ pounds Vegetables (page 229) (Pick 1 or more)
½ cup dry white wine
1 cup evaporated milk
1 cup good-quality vegetable broth
2 tablespoons olive oil
3 large garlic cloves, minced
3 tablespoons all-purpose flour
½ cup grated Parmesan cheese, plus extra for topping
Ground black or white pepper

Bring 2 quarts of water and 1 tablespoon salt to a boil in a large soup kettle. Add the pasta and, using back-of-the-box times as a guide, cook, partially covered and stirring frequently at first to prevent sticking, until just tender. If using **Firm Vegetables/Sturdy Greens,** add to the boiling pasta water for the last 5 or so minutes of cooking. Set a colander over a large bowl and drain the pasta (and vegetables), reserving the cooking liquid. Return the pasta to the pot.

Meanwhile, combine the wine, milk, and broth in a 1-quart glass measuring cup. Microwave until steamy hot, 3 to 4 minutes.

Heat the 2 tablespoons of oil in a large skillet over medium-high heat. If using **Tender Vegetables,** add them now and cook until tender, 5 to 7 minutes. Add the garlic and cook until fragrant and golden, about 1 minute. (If not using tender vegetables, simply heat the garlic with the oil.) Whisk in the flour and then vigorously whisk in the hot milk mixture. Simmer until the sauce is neither thin nor gloppy, a couple of minutes longer. Whisk in the ½ cup of Parmesan and season to taste with salt and pepper.

Add the sauce to the drained pasta, along with enough pasta cooking liquid to achieve the desired consistency; toss to coat. Adjust the seasonings. Serve sprinkled with a bit more Parmesan.

Serves 4

master formula veggie pasta with white wine sauce

Salt

12 ounces pasta (bite-size, linguine, fettuccine, or spaghetti)

1 to 1½ pounds Vegetables (page 229) (Pick 1 or more)

2 tablespoons pure olive oil

3 large garlic cloves, minced

½ teaspoon red pepper flakes

1 cup dry white wine

Add-Ins (Pick 1 or more; optional)

Fresh Herbs

½ cup grated Parmesan cheese, plus extra for topping

2 tablespoons extra-virgin olive oil

Salt and ground black pepper

Bring 2 quarts of water and 1 tablespoon salt to a boil in a large soup kettle. Add the pasta and, using back-of-the-box times as a guide, cook, partially covered and stirring frequently at first to prevent sticking, until just tender. If using Firm Vegetables/Sturdy Greens, add to the boiling pasta water for the last 5 or so minutes of cooking. Set a colander over a large bowl and drain the pasta (and vegetables), reserving the cooking liquid. Return the pasta to the pot.

Meanwhile, heat the olive oil in a large skillet over medium-high heat. If using Tender Vegetables, add them now and cook until crisp-tender, 5 to 7 minutes. Add the garlic and pepper flakes and cook until fragrant and golden, about 1 minute. (If not using tender vegetables, simply heat garlic and pepper flakes with the oil.) Add the wine and cook until reduced by half, a couple of minutes. Stir in the optional Add-Ins and the Fresh Herbs.

Add the sauce, ½ cup Parmesan, and extra-virgin olive oil to the drained pasta, tossing to coat. Add pasta cooking liquid as needed to create a light, flavorful sauce. Adjust the seasonings, including salt and pepper to taste. Serve sprinkled with additional Parmesan.

Add-Ins (Pick 1 or more; optional)
- 1 finely diced tomato or one 14.5-ounce can petite-cut diced tomatoes, drained
- 1 can (15.5 ounces) white beans, drained
- ⅓ cup coarsely chopped Kalamata or other piquant olives
- 2 tablespoons drained capers
- ¼ cup chopped fresh parsley or basil leaves
- ½ teaspoon dried (or 1½ teaspoons fresh) oregano or thyme leaves

Serves 4

master formula veggie pasta with creamy ricotta sauce

Salt

12 ounces pasta (bite-size, linguine, fettuccine, or spaghetti)

1 to ½ pounds Firm Vegetables/Sturdy Greens (page 229) (Pick 1 or more)

3 large garlic cloves, minced

Fresh Herbs (page 229) (Pick 1)

2 cups part-skim ricotta cheese

½ cup grated Parmesan cheese plus more for serving

Bring 2 quarts of water and 1 tablespoon salt to a boil in a large soup kettle. Add the pasta and, using back-of-the-box times as a guide, cook, partially covered and stirring frequently at first to prevent sticking, until just tender. Add Firm Vegetables/Sturdy Greens to the boiling pasta for the last 5 minutes of cooking. Set a colander over a large bowl and drain the pasta, reserving the cooking liquid. Return the pasta to the pot, stirring in the garlic and Fresh Herbs until fragrant. Stir in the ricotta, ½ cup Parmesan, and enough hot pasta cooking liquid to form a creamy sauce. Serve sprinkled with Parmesan.

Serves 4

master formula veggie pasta with presto pesto

Salt
12 ounces pasta (bite-size, linguine, fettuccine, or spaghetti)
1 to ½ pounds Firm Vegetables/Sturdy Greens (page 229) (Pick 1 or more)
2 large garlic cloves
¼ cup pine nuts
2 cups packed basil leaves
½ cup extra-virgin olive oil
¼ cup coarsely grated Parmesan, plus extra for topping
Ground black pepper

Bring 2 quarts of water and 1 tablespoon salt to a boil in a large soup kettle. Add the pasta and, using back-of-the-box times as a guide, cook, partially covered and stirring frequently at first to prevent sticking, until just tender. Add Firm Vegetables/Sturdy Greens to the boiling pasta for the last 5 minutes of cooking. Set a colander over a large bowl and drain the pasta, reserving the cooking liquid. Return the pasta to the pot.

Meanwhile, heat a small skillet over low heat. Add the whole garlic cloves and toast for 1 minute. Add the pine nuts and continue to heat, shaking the pan frequently until the nuts are golden and the garlic is spotty brown, about 4 minutes longer. Transfer to a plate to cool slightly.

Combine the garlic, nuts, and basil in a blender or food processor and mince. With the machine still running, gradually add the oil through the feed tube (or hole in the blender top) until the mixture is pureed. Transfer to a small bowl and stir in the ¼ cup Parmesan and salt and pepper to taste.

Add the pesto and enough pasta cooking liquid to the hot pasta for desired moistness; toss to coat. Adjust the seasoning, adding salt and several grinds of pepper. Serve sprinkled with additional Parmesan.

Serves 4

pam's fave combos for veggie pasta

Asparagus and Mushrooms with Light Alfredo Sauce

Butternut Squash with Creamy Ricotta Sauce

Thin Green Beans with Presto Pesto

Broccoli and Mushrooms with Creamy Tomato Sauce

Leeks and Green Peas with Light Alfredo Sauce

Cauliflower and Peppers in Light White Wine Sauce

Spinach with Creamy Ricotta Sauce

notes and tips

- If you're in a hurry or just want to make your pasta with a single vegetable, that's perfectly fine. But 2 vegetables, I think, are almost always more fun than 1. Instead of using all broccoli or mushrooms, for example, use a mix of broccoli and peppers, leeks and mushrooms, or butternut squash and kale (or even 3 vegetables like asparagus, carrots, and peas).

- I use a lot less water and a lot more salt to cook pasta than most cooks. Half the water means it heats twice as fast, and generously salting the water means the pasta actually tastes seasoned. As the pasta and vegetables cook, they release starch and flavor into the water. In a large pot of boiling water, this would be completely lost. In the smaller amount, however, it forms a light, flavorful vegetable broth, great for thinning sauces and tossing with pasta. ➤

- This pasta broth is also great for moistening leftovers. Pour leftover pasta onto a rimmed baking sheet to cool quickly and stop the cooking and save a cup or two of the pasta cooking water. When you're ready to reheat the pasta, microwave it on high or warm it stovetop over low heat, stirring in the reserved pasta cooking liquid to make it moist again.

- A dash of baking soda added to the tomato sauce prevents the evaporated milk from curdling. ➤

classy vegetable risotto

For years I've been using a shortcut oven method to make risotto, and while it's far less labor-intensive, without a watchful eye, the rice can overcook and get a little bloated. When it needs to be perfect, I've come to realize, there is no substitute for the time-honored method.

I recently cooked for friends. As we talked, I casually ladled in the broth and stirred. Between stirs I tossed and served the salad and poured the water and wine.

Could I have made the risotto ahead? Of course. Restaurant chefs par-cook it; I've got my own hands-free method. But the fact is, most of us don't need a shortcut. We just need a little time and a helping hand.

So whether you're having people over or just making supper, there's usually an eager kid, a budding cook, or just someone who's happy to help . . . if you just ask.

master formula classy vegetable risotto

1 quart good-quality vegetable broth
(I like Imagine No-Chicken Broth here)
Big pinch of saffron
2 tablespoons olive oil
2 heaping cups Vegetables*
(Pick 1 or more)
1 medium onion, cut into small dice
2 garlic cloves, minced
2 cups Arborio rice
1 cup dry white wine
Salt and ground black pepper
1 cup coarsely grated Parmesan cheese,
plus extra for topping
3 ounces cream cheese
Ground black or white pepper

Bring the broth and 2 cups of water to a simmer in a large saucepan over medium-high heat. Add the saffron and reduce the heat to low so the broth barely simmers.

Meanwhile, heat the oil over medium heat in a 5- to 6-quart Dutch oven or soup kettle. If using a Cetegory 1 Vegetable, add it and the onion and cook until golden and starting to brown, about 5 minutes. Add the garlic and stir until fragrant, 30 seconds, then add the rice and stir until well coated and toasted, a couple of minutes longer. Stir in the wine; simmer until almost evaporated, a couple of minutes longer. Knowing the process takes 20 to 25 minutes (I set a timer for 20), start adding broth to rice about $\frac{1}{2}$ cup at a time—stirring lazily at first and continuously toward the end—adding more only after rice has absorbed the previous amount, until rice is tender with a slight chew at the center. If using a Category 2 Vegetable, stir it in the last few minutes of cooking. If more than the suggested 6 cups of liquid is needed, stir in water, $\frac{1}{4}$ cup at a time, to achieve the desired consistency. Stir in cheeses and several grinds of pepper. Serve, sprinkling each portion with cheese.

Serves 6 as a hearty main course, 8 as a first course or light meal

Category 1 vegetables can stand up to longer cooking times, so they can be added at the outset. Those in Category 2 will lose their color and shape more quickly, so they should be briefly precooked then added just to heat through.

vegetable risotto options

Vegetables (Pick 1 or more)

Category 1 Vegetables

- **Winter squash—peeled and cut into ½-inch dice**
- **Fennel—stalks discarded, bulb halved lengthwise, cored, and thinly sliced**
- **Mushrooms—thinly sliced**
- **Cabbage—cored and thinly sliced**

Category 2 Vegetables (note that asparagus and broccoli require precooking)

- **Asparagus—tough ends snapped off, tips removed, spears halved lengthwise and cut crosswise into 1-inch lengths.** Before making the risotto, heat 2 teaspoons oil in the pot over high heat, add the asparagus tips and spears, and cook quickly until bright green and crisp-tender, 2 to 3 minutes. Spread out on a small rimmed baking pan in a single layer to stop the cooking.

- **Broccoli—cut into small florets, stems peeled and thinly sliced.** Before making the risotto, place the broccoli, ¼ cup water, 2 teaspoons oil, and a light sprinkling of salt in the pot. Cover and steam over high heat until the broccoli is bright green and crisp-tender, about 5 minutes. Spread out on a small rimmed baking sheet to stop the cooking.

- **Fresh or frozen corn**

- **Baby spinach or arugula** (note that 8 ounces will equal about 8 packed cups)

pam's faves for classy vegetable risotto

Broccoli

Butternut squash

Asparagus

Tomato and corn: Substitute 2 cups of tomato juice for the 2 cups of water added to the broth. Stir in ½ cup chopped fresh basil at the end.

Double mushroom: Heat 1 ounce (scant cup) coarsely chopped dried mushrooms in 2 cups water; let stand until soft, about 5 minutes. Strain and reserve mushrooms, adding enough water to broth to return it to 2 cups. Combine with the heated broth (omitting the 2 cups of water and the saffron). Stir in ¾ teaspoon dried thyme with the rice.

Spinach and lemon: Stir in 2 teaspoons finely grated lemon zest along with the cheeses.

notes and tips

- You can choose just one vegetable for your risotto, but you can mix it up too—mushrooms and broccoli or spinach and butternut squash. And regardless of the vegetable, you can always stir in 1 cup frozen green peas or 4 packed cups (about 4 ounces) baby spinach as a second vegetable toward the end of cooking.

- For my oven method, here are the basics: Sauté the onion, stir in the rice and the wine, add cold broth, cover tightly with heavy-duty foil, pressing the foil onto the surface of the rice and broth. Throw it in a 450°F oven. Twenty minutes or so later it emerges, ready for last-minute stirring and flavoring.

- Once the rice is toasted and opaque, it's time to start adding the liquid. Throughout the cooking process, ladle in the next addition when nearly all of the liquid has been absorbed. ➤

- The finished risotto should have a creamy, starchy sauce with a fairly loose consistency. Adding a few chunks of cream cheese to the finished risotto makes it extra rich and creamy. ➤

"meaty" asian stir-fries

I've been using some form of this stir-fry formula for nearly 2 decades. Over the years it's been tweaked, streamlined, updated. Now the formula's gone vegetarian, and it works for vegans too.

So what's new? I offer a host of "meaty" substitutes. Two are soybean based—extra-firm tofu and tempeh—that work as meatless protein. Seitan is made from wheat gluten that is formed into cutlets that can be sliced like meat and soaks up flavors like chicken. Mushrooms and eggplant offer meaty mouth-feel. Choose one of these as your stir-fry base, marinating it in a mix of soy and sherry as you would meat, poultry, or seafood.

Using a large, hot skillet to cook the sweet brown marinated base lets it brown beautifully and cook quickly, at which point it's turned out of the skillet to make sizzle room for the rest of the stir-fry.

Firm vegetables need a little moist heat to get tender, so they're flash-steamed in the skillet ahead of time. This precooking takes the stress off the skillet during the stir-fry process. Since they're nearly fully cooked beforehand, the firm vegetables get added back to the pan at the end—just long enough for them to heat through and to pick up the flavors of the aromatics and sauce. The tender vegetables get cooked—start to finish—during the stir-fry process.

All that's left at that point is choosing a sauce. They're all lively and highly seasoned, making them especially perfect meatless stir-fries. Serve with cooked white or brown rice.

master formula "meaty" asian stir-fry

8 ounces "Meaty" Substitute (Pick 1)
1 tablespoon soy sauce
1 tablespoon dry sherry
1 pound Vegetables (Pick 2 or 3)
Flavoring Sauces (Pick 1)
Salt
3 tablespoons peanut or vegetable oil
1 large onion, halved from pole to pole,
each half cut into 6 wedges
1 tablespoon minced garlic
1 tablespoon minced fresh ginger
2 teaspoons cornstarch mixed with
2 teaspoons water

Toss the "Meaty" Substitute with the soy sauce and sherry in a medium bowl; set aside. Prep all Vegetables and your Flavoring Sauce and arrange near the cooktop.

When ready to stir-fry, if using Firm Vegetables, combine them with a light sprinkling of salt and $\frac{1}{3}$ cup of water in a 12-inch skillet. Cover the pan and turn the heat on high. When the water starts to boil, set the timer and cook until crisp-tender, 2 to 4 minutes, depending on the vegetable.

Transfer the vegetables to a plate and return the skillet to high heat. Add 1 tablespoon of the oil and heat until wisps of smoke start to rise from the pan. Add the "Meaty Substitute," reserving any unabsorbed marinade in the bowl. Cook, turning once, until well browned and cooked through, 2 to 3 minutes. Return to the bowl with the marinade; set aside.

Drizzle another 1 tablespoon of the oil into the hot skillet. Add the onion and stir-fry until spotty brown and crisp, about 1 minute. If using Tender Vegetables, add them now and stir-fry until crisp-tender, 1 to 2 minutes.

Make a well in the middle of the skillet and add the remaining 1 tablespoon oil, the garlic, and ginger. Cook for a few seconds, until fragrant, and then toss together with the vegetables. Add the reserved steamed firm vegetables and cook until all the vegetables are crisp-tender, 1 to 2 minutes. Return the "meaty" substitute to the pan.

Stir in the Flavoring Sauce, tossing to coat all the ingredients. Stir the cornstarch mixture and add to the skillet; stir-fry until the juices become saucy and glossy, adding a tablespoon or 2 of water if too thick.

Serves 4

stir-fry options

"Meaty" Substitute (Pick 1)

- Tempeh—cut into bite-size pieces
- Seitan—pulled into bite-size shreds and patted dry
- Extra-firm tofu—pressed dry with a kitchen towel to remove as much moisture as possible and cut into bite-size cubes
- Baby bella (aka cremini) mushrooms—sliced
- Eggplant—cut crosswise into $\frac{1}{2}$-inch-thick slices and then halved or quartered, depending on the eggplant size

Vegetables (Pick 2 or 3, but not all from one category)

Tender Vegetables

- Bell peppers—stemmed, cored, and cut into bite-size strips
- Snow peas or sugar snap peas—strings removed, if necessary
- Celery—cut into $\frac{1}{2}$-inch-thick slices
- Zucchini or yellow squash—cut crosswise into $\frac{1}{2}$-inch-thick rounds (halve large rounds)

- Fresh bean sprouts
- Canned sliced water chestnuts—drained
- Canned baby corn, drained
- Fresh or juice-packed canned pineapple chunks—though not a vegetable, it makes for a tasty sweet-and-sour stir-fry

Firm Vegetables

- Thin asparagus—tough ends snapped off, stalks cut into 1-inch lengths
- Broccoli crowns—cut into bite-size florets, thinly slice stems
- Cauliflower—cut into bite-size florets
- Carrots—peeled and cut into $\frac{1}{4}$- to $\frac{1}{2}$-inch-thick slices
- Green cabbage—quartered, cored, and thickly shredded
- Thin green beans (haricots verts)—left whole
- Sweet potatoes—peeled and cut into thick slices (halve or even quarter if large)
- Butternut or other winter squash—peeled, seeded, and cut into thick slices, then into bite-size pieces

Flavoring Sauces (Pick 1)

- **General Tso's Stir-Fry Sauce:** Whisk together 6 tablespoons water, $\frac{1}{4}$ cup dark soy (or in a pinch 2 tablespoons *each* molasses and soy sauce), 2 tablespoons rice vinegar, 2 tablespoons sweet sherry, and $\frac{1}{2}$ teaspoon red pepper flakes

- **Spicy Orange Stir-Fry Sauce:** Whisk together $\frac{1}{4}$ cup water, 6 tablespoons orange juice concentrate, 2 tablespoons dark soy sauce (or in a pinch 1 tablespoon *each* soy sauce and molasses), 2 teaspoons toasted sesame oil, and $\frac{1}{2}$ teaspoon red pepper flakes

- **Coconut Curry Stir-Fry Sauce:** Whisk together $\frac{3}{4}$ cup light coconut milk, 2 tablespoons sweet sherry, 2 tablespoons soy sauce, and 1 tablespoon curry powder

- **Basil (or Cilantro) Stir-Fry Sauce:** Whisk together $\frac{1}{4}$ cup water, $\frac{1}{4}$ cup vegetable broth, $\frac{1}{4}$ cup soy sauce, 2 teaspoons rice vinegar, 1 teaspoon sugar, and $\frac{1}{3}$ cup chopped fresh basil or cilantro

- **Lemon-Coconut Stir-Fry Sauce:** Whisk together $\frac{1}{2}$ cup light coconut milk, 1 teaspoon grated lemon zest, 3 tablespoons lemon juice, 2 tablespoons soy sauce, 2 tablespoons sweet sherry, and 4 teaspoons brown sugar

- **Sweet and Sour Stir-Fry Sauce:** Whisk together 6 tablespoons pineapple juice, 3 tablespoons soy sauce, 3 tablespoons balsamic vinegar, $1\frac{1}{2}$ tablespoons brown sugar, and $\frac{1}{2}$ teaspoon red pepper flakes

- **Sichuan Chili Stir-Fry Sauce:** Whisk together $\frac{1}{4}$ cup water, 1 tablespoon soy sauce, 1 tablespoon toasted sesame oil, 2 tablespoons dark soy sauce (or in a pinch 1 tablespoon *each* soy sauce and molasses), 3 tablespoons sweet sherry, 2 tablespoons chili sauce, and $\frac{1}{2}$ teaspoon Sichuan peppercorns, crushed

notes and tips

- A successful stir-fry depends on having all your ingredients—your mise en place—prepped and arranged near the stove before you fire up the skillet. Once you're organized, the actual cooking takes just minutes. ➤

- You can pick several vegetables to make up the 1 pound, but choose at least one from each category to keep the skillet from becoming overburdened.

- Stir-frying the onion wedges by themselves means they will turn spotty brown very quickly. ➤

asian rice and noodle dishes

Although the technique for each of the dishes in this section is slightly different, the principles behind the first three—Veggie Lo Mein, Simple Fried Rice, and Perfect Pad Thai—are the same: Get the skillet blistering hot. (You will probably want to turn on the vent fan if you have one because the hot pan will create some smoke when the ingredients hit the surface.) Don't overcrowd the pan. You want these dishes to sizzle aggressively, not gently stew—which is why they cook in two stages.

Vegetables first—added sequentially a minute or two apart—to keep the stir-fry momentum going. Still crisp-tender, they're transferred to a plate to make room for the pasta, rice, or noodles that stir-fry equally quickly. In a flash, the vegetables return to the skillet for a quick heat-through before it's time to serve up.

What time these dishes take in prep is made up once you get to the stove. With a good hot pan, the cooking process takes just 6 to 8 minutes. If you start heating your skillet on low when you first walk into the kitchen, it can come up to temperature in no time when you're ready to cook.

Unlike the first three dishes, the technique for Noodles and Veggies with Thai Peanut Sauce is akin to the Supper Pasta Formulas (page 225). Here you cook the firm vegetables along with the pasta in the pot of boiling water and sauté the tender vegetables in the pan along with the sauce and toss the two with a little pasta cooking water.

master formula veggie lo mein

8 ounces extra-firm tofu, cut into
bite-size cubes, or shredded seitan

Salt

8 ounces Firm Vegetables (Pick 1)

8 ounces spaghetti or lo mein noodles

1 tablespoon soy sauce

2 tablespoons vegetable oil

1 medium-large onion, halved from pole
to pole, each half cut into 6 wedges

8 ounces Tender Vegetables (Pick 1)

1 tablespoon minced garlic

1 tablespoon minced fresh ginger

Lo Mein Sauce (recipe follows)

Drain the tofu and place on a plate. Top with a second plate and weight with a heavy can. Set aside for 10 minutes to press out some of the liquid.

Bring 2 quarts of water and a generous sprinkling of salt to a boil in a large pot. Add the Firm Vegetable and cook until crisp-tender, about 2 minutes. Transfer to a plate with a slotted spoon. Add the pasta to the pot and cook, stirring frequently, until just tender; drain and set aside.

Cut the tofu in bite-size cubes and toss with the soy.

Meanwhile, heat a 12-inch nonstick skillet over high heat until very hot. Add 1 tablespoon of the oil and the onion; stir-fry until crisp and spotty brown, about 1 minute. Add the Tender Vegetable and stir-fry until just cooked, about 2 minutes. Add the tofu and stir-fry until lightly browned, about 1 minute. Add the cooked firm vegetable and stir-fry until heated through, about 1 minute. Add the garlic and ginger and stir-fry until fragrant, about 30 seconds. Transfer everything to a plate.

Add the remaining 1 tablespoon oil to the empty skillet and heat until shimmering. Add the pasta and stir-fry until heated through, about 2 minutes. Return the vegetable mixture to the pan, along with the Lo Mein Sauce, stirring to coat. Serve hot.

Serves 4

lo mein options

Firm Vegetables (Pick 1)

- Asparagus—tough ends snapped off, spears cut into 1-inch lengths
- Snow peas or sugar snap peas—strings removed if necessary
- Broccoli or cauliflower—cut into small florets
- Carrots—peeled and thinly sliced
- White turnips or rutabaga (yellow turnip)—peeled and cut into small dice
- Butternut or other winter squash—peeled and cut into small dice
- Thin green beans—cut into 1½-inch lengths

Tender Vegetables (Pick 1)

- Zucchini or yellow squash—halved lengthwise and thinly sliced crosswise (if squash is small, no need to halve)
- Baby bella (aka cremini) mushrooms—sliced
- Bell peppers—stemmed, cored, and cut into bite-size strips
- Eggplant—quartered lengthwise and thinly sliced crosswise (if eggplant is small, halve; if using Japanese variety, simply slice)
- Fennel—stalks discarded, bulb halved, cored, and thinly sliced
- Cabbage or bok choy—cored and finely shredded
- Bean sprouts

lo mein sauce

¼ cup vegetable broth
¼ cup soy sauce
2 teaspoons rice vinegar
2 teaspoons toasted sesame oil
1 teaspoon red pepper flakes
1 teaspoon sugar

Whisk all ingredients together.

Makes ½ cup

master formula simple fried rice

7 to 8 ounces extra-firm tofu
4 tablespoons low-sodium soy sauce
8 ounces Category 1 Vegetables* (Pick 1)
8 ounces Category 2 Vegetables* (Pick 1)
4 tablespoons vegetable oil
1 medium-large onion, halved from pole
to pole, each half cut into 6 wedges
1 tablespoon minced garlic
4 cups cooked brown or white rice
2 large eggs, beaten
4 scallions, thinly sliced

Drain the tofu and place on a plate. Top with a second plate and weight with a heavy can. Set aside for 10 minutes to press out some of the liquid. Cut into bite-size cubes and marinate in 1 tablespoon of the soy sauce.

Prepare the Vegetables and place them in separate bowls near the stove.

A few minutes before you are ready to start cooking, turn on vent fan and heat a 12-inch nonstick skillet over high heat until very hot. Add 1 tablespoon of the oil and the onion and stir-fry until crisp and spotty brown, about 1 minute. Add the Category 1 Vegetable and stir-fry until crisp-tender, 1 to 2 minutes. Add the tofu and stir-fry until lightly browned, about 1 minute. Add the Category 2 Vegetable and stir-fry until crisp-tender, about 1 minute. Stir in the garlic, then transfer the mixture to a plate and set aside.

Add the remaining 3 tablespoons oil to the skillet and heat until shimmering. Add the rice and stir-fry, breaking up the clumps, until heated through, about 2 minutes. Add the eggs and stir-fry until scrambled, about 1 minute. Return the vegetable/tofu mixture, along with the remaining 3 tablespoons soy sauce and the scallions, stirring to combine. Serve hot.

Category 1 vegetables are those that go directly into the stir-fry from a raw state. Category 2 vegetables are those that either are fully cooked (canned water chestnuts), need to be steamed before going into the skillet, or cook in a flash, like bean sprouts.

Serves 4

fried rice options

Category 1 Vegetables (Pick 1)

- Celery—thinly sliced
- Fennel—stalks discarded, bulb halved, cored, and thinly sliced
- Bell pepper—stemmed, cored, and cut into bite-size strips
- Sliced mushrooms
- Eggplant—cut into medium-small dice
- Zucchini or yellow squash—cut into medium-small dice

Category 2 Vegetables (Pick 1)

- Canned sliced water chestnuts—drained
- Bean sprouts
- Broccoli crowns—cut into florets, stalks thinly sliced, both lightly steamed)
- Carrots—peeled, thinly sliced, and lightly steamed
- Pencil-thin asparagus—cut into 1-inch lengths and lightly steamed
- Snow peas or sugar snap peas—strings removed if necessary and lightly steamed

Note: To lightly steam broccoli, carrots, asparagus, or peas, place the vegetable and ⅓ cup of water in the skillet you'll be using for the fried rice. Cover and turn the burner on high. The vegetable should be crisp-tender in about 3 minutes.

perfect
pad thai

If you can't find Thai rice stick noodles, substitute an equal amount of cooked spaghetti (8 ounces dry or 4 cups cooked).

7 to 8 ounces extra-firm tofu
   (½ package)
8 ounces Thai rice stick noodles
Pad Thai Sauce (recipe follows)
1 medium-large onion, halved from pole to
   pole, each half cut into 6 wedges
1 tablespoon minced garlic
6 scallions, cut into 1-inch lengths
8 ounces (scant 3 cups) bean sprouts, rinsed
2 large eggs, lightly beaten
2 tablespoons vegetable oil
1 lime, cut into 6 wedges
¼ cup roasted peanuts, coarsely chopped
Cilantro leaves, for garnish (optional)

Drain the tofu and place on a plate. Top with a second plate and weight with a heavy can. Set aside for 10 minutes to press out some of the liquid.

Place the noodles in an 8- or 9-inch square pan; add boiling water to cover (about 6 cups). Cover and let stand until soft, about 5 minutes. Drain and set aside.

Place the Pad Thai Sauce in a small bowl. Cut the pressed tofu in bite-size cubes. Arrange the onion, garlic, scallions, bean sprouts, and eggs next to your stovetop.

Three to 4 minutes before starting to cook, heat a 12-inch nonstick skillet over high heat. Add 1 tablespoon of the oil and the onion and stir-fry until the onion is still crisp and spotty brown,

about 1 minute. Add the tofu and stir-fry until lightly browned, about 1 minute. Stir in the garlic, scallions, and bean sprouts and stir-fry until the vegetables wilt slightly, about 1 minute. Make a well in the center of the pan and pour in the eggs. Cook until partially set, then scramble into the vegetable mixture. Transfer to a bowl, pour half the Pad Thai Sauce over it, and toss to coat.

Add the remaining 1 tablespoon oil to the same skillet and heat until shimmering. Toss the noodles with the remaining Pad Thai sauce. Add to the skillet and stir-fry until heated through, about 2 minutes. Return the vegetable mixture to the skillet and stir-fry with the noodles until heated through. Transfer to a serving platter; squeeze 2 of the lime wedges over the noodles, sprinkle with peanuts, and garnish with cilantro and remaining lime wedges. Serve immediately.

Serves 4

pad thai sauce

6 tablespoons low-sodium soy sauce (or
   Vietnamese fish sauce if not a strict
   vegetarian)
2 tablespoons sugar
1 teaspoon red pepper flakes

Mix all ingredients together.

Makes ⅓ cup

master formula noodles & veggies with thai peanut sauce

¾ cup light coconut milk
¼ cup peanut butter
2 tablespoons soy sauce
2 teaspoons brown sugar
Salt
12 ounces spaghetti, linguine, or fettuccine
1 pound Vegetables (Pick 1 or more)
1 to 2 tablespoons vegetable oil
1 tablespoon minced garlic
1 tablespoon minced fresh ginger
½ teaspoon red pepper flakes
Garnishes: thinly sliced scallions, chopped fresh cilantro, chopped peanuts

Whisk together the coconut milk, peanut butter, soy sauce, and brown sugar in a small bowl and set aside.

Bring 2 quarts of water and 1 tablespoon of salt to boil in a large soup kettle. Add the pasta and, using back-of-the-box times as a guide, cook, partially covered and stirring frequently at first to prevent sticking, until just tender. If using **Firm Vegetables/Sturdy Greens,** add to the boiling pasta for the last 5 minutes or so of cooking. Set a colander over a large bowl. Drain the pasta, reserving the cooking liquid; return the pasta to the pot.

Meanwhile, heat 2 tablespoons of oil in a large skillet. If using **Tender Vegetables,** add them now and cook until crisp-tender, 5 to 7 minutes. Add the garlic, ginger, and pepper flakes and cook until fragrant and golden, about 1 minute. (If not using tender vegetables, use only 1 tablespoon of oil to cook the garlic, ginger, and pepper flakes.) Add the peanut sauce, bring to a simmer, and remove from the heat; set aside until the pasta is done.

Add the contents of the skillet to the drained pasta, tossing to coat and adding pasta cooking liquid as necessary to create a light, flavorful sauce. Adjust the seasonings. Serve sprinkled with any or all of the suggested garnishes.

Serves 4

thai noodle options

Vegetables (Pick 1 or more)

Firm Vegetables/Sturdy Greens

- Asparagus—tough stalks snapped off, spears cut into 1-inch lengths
- Snow peas or sugar snap peas—strings removed if necessary
- Fresh or frozen green peas—no more than 1 cup and use with a mix of vegetables
- Broccoli or cauliflower—cut into florets
- Carrots—peeled and thinly sliced
- White turnips or rutabaga (yellow turnip)—peeled and cut into small dice
- Butternut or other winter squash—peeled and cut into small dice
- Thin green beans—cut into $1\frac{1}{2}$-inch lengths
- Spinach—stemmed if needed
- Bok choy—cored and thinly sliced crosswise
- Beet greens, Swiss chard, kale, collards, turnip greens—stemmed and coarsely chopped

Tender Vegetables

- Zucchini or yellow squash—halved lengthwise and thinly sliced crosswise
- Baby bella (aka cremini) mushrooms—sliced
- Bell peppers—stemmed, cored, and thinly sliced
- Eggplant—quartered lengthwise and thinly sliced crosswise
- Fennel—stalks discarded, bulb halved, cored, and thinly sliced
- Cabbage—cored and thinly sliced
- Onions (red, white, or yellow)—halved and thinly sliced crosswise
- Leeks—white and light green parts only, quartered lengthwise, cut into medium dice, and well washed

pam's fave combos for noodles and veggies

Bok choy and bell peppers

Broccoli and mushrooms

Butternut squash and cabbage

Spinach and leeks

Cauliflower and eggplant

six-at-a-time main course quesadillas

Light snack meets grilled cheese: That's how quesadillas always struck me. Easy enough, I thought, to turn them into a serious main course. But I quickly discovered that bulking up the filling tends to wreak havoc with the tortilla and that you end up with a limp, over-stuffed quesadilla.

For quesadillas to make it as dinner material, the cooking process needed to shift from one-at-a-time stovetop to six-at-a-time in the oven. And they still needed that appealing crisp exterior with a substantial but relatively dry interior.

Here's how to do it. As you move into the kitchen, set a medium skillet and a large skillet on low heat, adjust the oven rack to the lowest position, and preheat the oven to 400°F. Pick and prep one of the suggested five vegetables. You may not have kale or zucchini, but surely you've got an onion, a pepper, or maybe a little chunk of cabbage hanging out. For your base ingredient, choose from these four options: corn, pinto beans, black beans, and hominy. (I love hominy.)

Turn the heat up on the large skillet and sauté the vegetable, which takes only about 4 minutes. Add garlic, cumin, and oregano and cook for a few seconds, then add the base and cook it just enough to evaporate its moisture—a minute max. That's your filling.

Now turn up the heat on the medium skillet and start crisping up the flour tortillas one at a time, folding them as soon as they come out of the skillet and setting them on a baking sheet.

Now fill them—a little cheese, a little filling, some scallions and cilantro (optional, but I like it), and a final sprinkling of cheese. While they bake for 15 minutes, make a salad and mix the salsa and sour cream topping.

No one will miss the meat at this meal. Guaranteed.

master formula six-at-a-time main course quesadillas

2 tablespoons pure olive oil
8 ounces **Vegetables** (Pick 1)
2 large garlic cloves, minced
1 teaspoon ground cumin
$\frac{1}{2}$ teaspoon dried oregano
Base (Pick 1)
6 medium (8-inch) flour tortillas
$1\frac{1}{2}$ cups **Cheese** (Pick 1)
$\frac{1}{4}$ cup chopped fresh cilantro
$\frac{1}{4}$ cup sliced scallion greens
$\frac{1}{2}$ cup prepared salsa or salsa verde
1 cup reduced-fat sour cream
or 2% yogurt

Adjust the oven rack to the lowest position and preheat the oven to 400°F.

Place a medium skillet over low heat.

Meanwhile, heat the oil in a large skillet over medium-high heat. Add the **Vegetable** and cook until soft and starting to color, 4 to 5 minutes. Add the garlic, cumin, and oregano and cook until fragrant, about 30 seconds. Add the **Base** and cook until the mixture is dry and is just starting to stick to the pan, about 1 minute longer. Transfer to a plate and set aside.

Turn the heat under the medium skillet to medium-high. When wisps of smoke start to rise from the pan, add a tortilla and cook until spotty brown, about 30 seconds on the first side and 15 seconds on the second side; fold in half immediately and place on a large (18 x 12-inch) rimmed baking sheet. Repeat with the remaining tortillas. You should be able to fit 3 rows of 2 on the baking sheet.

Divide half the **Cheese** among the tortillas, opening each tortilla carefully and sprinkling it over the bottom half. Top with filling (a scant $\frac{1}{3}$ cup) and sprinkle with cilantro and scallions and then the remaining cheese. Press the folded tortillas lightly.

Bake the quesadillas until heated through and crisp, about 15 minutes. Cut each into 4 triangles and serve with salsa or salsa verde mixed with the sour cream.

Serves 3 to 6

quesadilla options

Vegetables (Pick 1)

- Onion—1 large, halved and thinly sliced
- Bell pepper (any color)—1 large, stemmed, cored, and cut into short, thin strips
- Zucchini—2 medium-small, cut into medium dice
- Cabbage—¼ small head, cored and thinly sliced (a heaping 2 cups)
- Tough greens, such as kale, turnip greens, collard greens—stemmed, washed, and coarsely chopped (8 packed cups)

Base (Pick 1)

- Pinto beans—1 can (15.5 ounces), drained
- Black beans—1 can (15.5 ounces), drained
- Frozen corn—8 ounces (about 2 cups), thawed
- Hominy—1 can (15.5 ounces), drained

Cheese (Pick 1)

- Sharp Cheddar, grated
- Pepper Jack, grated
- Monterey Jack, grated
- Queso fresco, crumbled

- Pan-toast the tortillas briefly before assembling the quesadillas to add color and make them pliable. ➤

pam's fave combos for six-at-a-time main course quesadillas

Onions and pinto beans with pepper or Monterey Jack

Peppers and corn with pepper Jack

Swiss chard and hominy with queso fresco

Zucchini and corn with pepper Jack

Cabbage and black beans with sharp Cheddar

taco bar sin carne

When my daughters were young their favorite meal was tacos. In fact, it was the first dinner the two of them ever made by themselves. They liked it because it tasted good, of course, but what they really liked was the colorful array of toppings and the freedom to assemble their own meal.

Although the toppings varied, depending on what was around, the well-spiced meat base was always there. But even that has evolved over the years. When the girls were really young, I made it with ground beef. In their angsty teen years when they were flirting with vegetarianism, I switched to ground turkey as a compromise.

When Maggy got married and started cooking for herself, she discovered fish tacos and got us all hooked as well. And now here I am, part-time vegetarian myself, and lentils are my new base.

I got the idea for lentils because I had already discovered they were a stellar stand-in for ground beef in Meatless Sloppy Joes (page 158). Other beans can work as a taco filling, but lentils are especially perfect because they best mimic ground meat. Lentils also don't require presoaking, and they cook in minutes. With my shallow-cook method, the lentils come to boil very quickly. After that they're perfectly cooked in about 15 minutes.

There are lots of reasons to use lentils as a taco filling. Besides the obvious—it's good for both us and the animals—it's economical too. A pound of lentils costs less than a buck and yields 6 cups of filling. A pound of ground beef is about $3 and yields less than 2 cups—three times the price, a third the yield. Plus, every time I make lentil tacos, my steak-loving midwestern husband never fails to say, "Who needs meat in these?"

master formula taco bar

2 to 3 hard taco shells and/or 6-inch
  flour tortillas per person
Chili Lentils for Tacos (page 266)
Fresh Ingredients (Pick 1 or more)
Rich Ingredients (Pick 1 or more)
Dairy (Pick 1 or both)
Finishers (Pick 1 or all)

Follow package instructions for heating hard
tacos. Heat flour tortillas as follows: Adjust the
oven rack to the middle position and preheat
the oven to 350°F. Lay a damp paper towel on a
24 x 18-inch piece of heavy-duty foil. Set 2
stacks of 4 corn tortillas on the damp towel.
Cover with another damp paper towel. Close
the foil to completely seal. Bake until steamy
hot, about 5 minutes.

Arrange bowls of Chili Lentils, the Fresh
Ingredient(s), Rich Ingredient(s), Dairy, and
Finishers on a tray or the center of your table,
along with a plate of warm taco shells or
tortillas. Allow each diner to assemble 2 or 3
tacos to their liking.

Serves 4

taco bar options

Fresh Ingredients (Pick 1 or more)

- Quick Cabbage Slaw (below)—As a topping or an accompaniment. If you're considering slaw a topping, you don't necessarily need more items from this category. If making the slaw an accompaniment, however, you may want to pick 1 or 2 more from here (and preferably not lettuce or onions, which are similar to the slaw).
- Romaine lettuce hearts—2 cups shredded, lightly salted just before serving
- Tomatoes—1 cup finely chopped, lightly salted
- Bell peppers—about 1 cup finely diced
- Onion—about ½ cup finely diced
- Radishes—about ½ cup halved and sliced

Rich Ingredients (Pick 1 or more)

- Guacamole—mash the flesh of 1 avocado, seasoning liberally with salt and lime juice
- Frozen corn—about 1 cup, microwaved until warm
- Ripe black, green, or pimiento-stuffed olives—about ½ cup sliced

Dairy (Pick 1 or both)

- Light sour cream—about ½ cup
- Cheese—generous 4 ounces grated sharp Cheddar, pepper Jack, or Monterey Jack or crumbled queso fresco

Finishers (I like all three)

- Salsa and/or salsa verde—1 cup
- Scallion greens—¼ cup sliced
- Cilantro—¼ cup chopped

quick cabbage slaw

4 cups finely grated cabbage (about ¼ small head)
¼ red onion, thinly sliced
2 tablespoons pure olive oil
Salt and ground black pepper
1 tablespoon rice vinegar

Toss the cabbage and red onion with the oil and a generous sprinkling of salt and pepper in a medium bowl, making sure the cabbage is lightly coated. Drizzle with the vinegar and toss to coat again. Adjust the seasonings, adding more vinegar, salt, and pepper to taste.

Makes scant 2 cups

chili lentils for tacos

1 pound brown lentils
2 tablespoons vegetable oil
1 large onion, chopped
3 large garlic cloves
¼ cup chili powder
2 teaspoons ground cumin
1 teaspoon dried oregano
1 can (14.5 ounces) petite-cut diced tomatoes
Salt and ground black pepper

Bring 5 cups of water and the lentils to a boil in a covered 12-inch skillet. Reduce the heat to medium and cook until the water is almost absorbed and the lentils are just tender, about 12 minutes. Turn off the heat.

Meanwhile, heat the oil in a Dutch oven over medium-high heat. Add the onion and cook until tender, about 5 minutes. Add the garlic, chili powder, cumin, and oregano and cook until fragrant, about 30 seconds. Add the cooked lentils and tomatoes. Reduce the heat to medium-low and cook until most of the liquid has evaporated, about 5 minutes. Adjust the seasoning, including a generous sprinkling of salt and pepper.

Makes about 6 cups

notes and tips

- A word about taco shells. You've got a choice of hard corn tortillas or soft flour tortillas. Even if they're oversize or the wide varieties that stand on their own, I find corn tortillas confining (I can never fit as much as I want in them) and more like a snack than an entrée. I usually offer a mix of flour tortillas and taco shells, but if I had to choose one, especially for dinner, I'd go with flour tortillas.

- Enjoy the slaw as a salad along with your tacos or use it as a taco filling. There are lots of other things you can add to this slaw—a handful of sliced radishes, a grated carrot, a bit of thin sliced bell pepper, a tablespoon or so of chopped cilantro—but if you're looking for a quick bang-it-out salad, here it is.

- The lentil mixture cooks so quickly that you might still be assembling taco bar ingredients when they're done. No worries. Just turn off the burner, cover the pot, and let them sit for a few minutes. In fact, a little rest time gives them a chance to soften a bit more—even better.

- You'll have more lentils than you need for tacos for 4, but they can be refrigerated for up to 5 days, and they freeze well too. Use the leftovers to make taco salad, nachos, or quesadillas. ➤

appendix

Cooking Grains and Legumes

Grains

Cooked grains refrigerate and freeze beautifully, so I've made the yield 4 cups, or enough for a salad made of a single grain. Since you'll more likely be using a mix of beans and grains for your salads, you'll have leftovers for a second salad (or even a soup or side dish) another time. Cooked grains can be refrigerated for several days or frozen for several months.

Brown rice, store-bought cooked—The quickest way to get 4 cups of cooked brown rice is to buy 2 packages (8 ounces each) plain cooked brown rice. Since it's fully cooked, it's an instant salad base. You will find it in the grocery aisle or freezer case.

Brown rice, instant whole-grain—Instant whole-grain brown rice is another quick fix. Simply bring $2\frac{1}{2}$ cups water and 1 teaspoon salt to a boil in a 5- to 6-quart Dutch oven or large saucepan. Add 3 cups instant whole-grain brown rice, bring to a simmer, cover, and cook for 5 minutes. Remove from the heat and let stand, covered, until tender, about 5 minutes longer.

Brown rice, traditionally cooked—Bring 4 cups water and 1 teaspoon salt to a boil in a 5- to 6-quart Dutch oven or large saucepan. Add 2 cups brown rice and bring to a simmer. Cover and cook over medium-low heat until tender, about 45 minutes.

White rice, store-bought cooked—You can buy plain cooked rice. There's 2 cups in an 8-ounce package.

White rice, traditionally cooked—For legume and grain salads, I prefer cooking rice so that it comes out dry and fluffy. To cook it this way, rinse 2 cups long- or medium-grain rice in a

large saucepan under cold running water. Drain, return the rice to the pan, add 3 cups water, cover, and bring to a boil. Reduce the heat to low and simmer 15 minutes. Remove from the heat and let stand, covered, 5 minutes longer.

Quinoa (red, white, or a mix)—For added flavor, toast the quinoa first. Place $1\frac{3}{4}$ cups quinoa in a 5- to 6-quart Dutch oven and toast over medium-high heat, stirring occasionally. When the quinoa starts to pop, stir constantly until it smells nutty and looks golden, 2 to 3 minutes longer. Add $3\frac{1}{2}$ cups water and 1 teaspoon salt. Bring to a simmer, cover, and cook over medium-low heat until just tender, about 15 minutes.

Barley, overnight method—My favorite way to cook barley. For 4 cooked cups, soak $1\frac{2}{3}$ cups barley in 4 cups water for 6 hours or overnight. Drain and transfer to a large saucepan. Add $1\frac{2}{3}$ cups water to the soaked barley and bring to a boil. Reduce to a simmer, cover, and cook until the water is absorbed and barley is tender, about 10 minutes. Turn off the heat and let stand, covered, for another 5 minutes.

Barley, traditional method—Bring 6 cups water and $1\frac{1}{2}$ teaspoons salt to a boil over medium-high heat in a large saucepan. Add $1\frac{1}{2}$ cups barley, cover, reduce heat to medium-low, and simmer, partially covered, until just tender, about 40 minutes.

Bulgur—Add $3\frac{1}{2}$ cups boiling water to $1\frac{1}{2}$ cups bulgur in a heatproof medium bowl. Cover and let stand until the water has almost all been absorbed, about 45 minutes.

Pasta, bite-size (whole-grain or regular)—The shape determines the yield, but you won't go too far wrong by bringing 2 quarts water and 1 tablespoon salt to a boil in a Dutch oven or soup kettle. Add 8 ounces pasta and, following the package times as a guide, cook until just tender. Drain and turn onto a rimmed baking sheet to cool. (Do not run under cold running water.)

Couscous, regular—Add 1¾ cups boiling water and 1 teaspoon salt to 1⅓ cups couscous in a large heatproof bowl. Cover with plastic wrap and let stand until the water has completely absorbed, about 7 minutes.

Couscous, Israeli—Place 2 cups Israeli couscous in a 5- to 6-quart Dutch oven. Toast the couscous over medium-high heat, stirring occasionally. When it starts to pop, stir constantly until it smells nutty and looks golden, 2 to 3 minutes longer. Add 4½ cups water and 1 teaspoon salt. Bring to a simmer, cover, and cook over medium-low heat until just tender, about 15 minutes.

Millet—Cook exactly as for barley.

Wheatberries, farro, spelt—Cook exactly as for barley.

Legumes

Beans—To cook 1 pound dried beans (which yields about 6 cups cooked beans), soak them in 6 cups water at least 6 hours or overnight. To speed up the process, pour 6 cups of boiling water over the dried beans. Soaked this way, they should be ready to cook in an hour or so. Drain and transfer the soaked beans to a large soup kettle. Add 2 quarts fresh water and bring to a simmer over medium-high heat. Reduce the heat to medium-low and cook until just tender, about 1 hour. When the beans have fully softened, season generously with salt. You can store the beans in their cooking liquid, but drain before using.

Lentils—Canned lentils are not common, though they do exist. The good news is that cooking lentils from scratch is easy; they don't need soaking and they cook in about 15 minutes. To cook 1 pound lentils (which yields about 6 cups), combine 5 cups water and 1 pound lentils in a covered 12-inch skillet and bring to a boil. Reduce the heat to medium and cook until the water is almost absorbed and the lentils are just tender, about 12 minutes.

Cooking Vegetables

For use in green or grain salads, on pizzas, in quesadillas, and in other recipes that call for precooked vegetables, follow the guidelines below.

Asparagus—Snap tough ends off, cut spears into 1-inch lengths (and halve lengthwise if thick). Steam/sauté by placing in a 12-inch skillet with ¾ cup of water, 1 tablespoon oil, and a sprinkling of salt and pepper. Cover and bring to a boil over high heat. Once the water boils, steam/sauté until just tender, 3 to 5 minutes. Drain. (A prepared bunch should yield a generous 2 cups.)

For a smokier, roasted flavor, toss with 2 teaspoons olive oil and a sprinkling of salt and pepper. Arrange in a single layer on a rimmed baking sheet; broil until tender-crisp, about 5 minutes.

Beets—Place scrubbed beets in a saucepan with water to cover, bring to a boil, and boil gently for 25 minutes, or until tender. Cool completely, then peel and slice or cube. A medium beet will yield about ¾ cup of ½-inch cubes.

If you have more time, you can roast the beets: Trim stems to half an inch and individually wrap in foil. Roast at 425°F for 50 minutes or until easily pierced with the tip of a knife. Cool completely, then peel (the skins will slip off easily) and slice or cube.

Bell peppers—Roast whole peppers under the broiler for 10 minutes, turning every 2 minutes or so until blackened all over. Cool, then rub off the charred skin. Slice off the stem end and pull out the core; discard. Slice the pepper open into a long, flat sheet and cut into strips or dice as needed.

Alternatively, stem and core raw peppers. Slice the pepper open into a long flat sheet and cut into thin strips. Sauté in a 12-inch skillet with 1 tablespoon oil until softened; cover and cook over low heat an additional 5 to 8 minutes or until very tender.

Broccoli and cauliflower florets—Steam/sauté 4 heaping cups as for asparagus, cooking 5 to 7 minutes. Drain and turn onto a baking sheet to stop cooking.

Fennel, cabbage—halve, core, and quarter if needed; thinly slice crosswise. Steam/sauté as for broccoli, cooking 7 to 9 minutes. Alternatively, cut in ¼-thick slices and roast as for root vegetables.

Greens (spinach, chard, kale, escarole, mustard or beet greens)—Remove tough center stems and slice leaves crosswise into ½-inch ribbons. Rinse very well and transfer to a 12-inch skillet with plenty of water still clinging to the leaves. Turn heat to high and wilt the greens, turning to expose all the leaves to the surface of the pan. Tender greens like spinach are done when they are all evenly wilted; cover the pan and cook sturdy greens until tender, 3 to 4 minutes for beet greens and chard, 5 to 8 minutes for kale and escarole, adding more water to the pan if it becomes dry. Cool and gently squeeze out any remaining moisture.

Green beans, sugar snap peas, or snow peas—Trim ends and halve or cut into 1-inch pieces if desired. Steam/sauté as for asparagus, cooking 3 to 4 minutes. Turn onto a baking sheet to stop cooking.

Onions—Thinly slice and broil as for zucchini, or sauté as for bell peppers, cooking up to 20 to 25 minutes, or until deep, golden brown, for caramelized onions.

Root vegetables (turnips, rutabagas, parsnips, potatoes)—Peel and cut into medium dice. If you're in a hurry, steam/sauté as for asparagus, using 1 cup of water, until just tender, 5 to 7 minutes. Drain.

If you have a more time, roast the root vegetables by tossing them with 1½ tablespoons olive oil and a sprinkling of salt and pepper. Turn them onto a baking sheet large enough for them to fit in a single layer. Roast at 450°F until tender, stirring once, 20 to 25 minutes.

Winter squash—peel, seed, and cut into small dice. Follow either cooking method for root vegetables.

Zucchini and yellow squash—Slice thinly and toss up to 4 heaping cups with 2 teaspoons olive oil and a sprinkling of salt and pepper. Arrange in a single layer on a rimmed baking sheet. Broil until spotty brown and just tender, about 5 minutes.

Toasting Nuts and Coconut

To toast ¼ cup nuts, place them in a small skillet over medium-low heat, shaking or stirring frequently, until fragrant and deeper in color, about 5 minutes. Transfer to a plate to cool. To toast larger quantities, place the nuts in a 9-inch square baking pan and roast in a 325°F oven, stirring once or twice, until fragrant and slightly deeper in color, 7 to 12 minutes, depending on the size of the nuts.

To toast coconut, spread 1 cup sweetened flaked coconut evenly in a single layer in a 9-inch square baking pan. Bake in a 300°F oven, stirring once or twice, until fragrant and golden, about 20 minutes.

acknowledgments

Thanks to Pam Krauss, my new editor, for believing in the Cook without a Book meatless approach to life. For producing such a beautiful, approachable book, thanks to the photography team of Quentin Bacon, assistant Lauren Volo, and prop stylist Natasha Louise King; and the food styling team of Cyd McDowell, supported by Vivian Lui, and Molly Shuster. Thank you all for such a memorable week.

Thanks to videographer Renee Bevan for so enthusiastically capturing *Cook without a Book: Meatless Meals* on film; Kara Plikaitis for her art direction and the team at Subtitle for their lovely design; production editor Zachary Greenwald; copy editor Kate Slate; Sarah Jane Freymann, cherished agent and friend through seven books and fifteen years; *USA Weekend,* for our more than a decade relationship; my new friends at AARP—thanks for making me your food expert; and *Runner's World,* for making me one of your regular running foodies (or would that be foodie runners?); David Anderson, partner on the less-meat, better-meat journey and gifted editor of ThreeManyCooks. com; and Andy Keet and Tony Damelio, sons-in-law present and future, for loving *all* of us and for generously tolerating Three Many Cooks.

index

Boldfaced page references indicate photographs.